from the
COAL MINES

to the
BOARD ROOM

Reflections on the Rise of Black
Politicians in Palm Beach County

Addie L. Greene

©2018 Addie L. Greene
All rights reserved

ISBN 978-0-9837566-0-6

Library of Congress Control Number 2018949136

No part of this book may be reproduced, stored in a retrieval system, or transmitted in any form or by any means, electronic, mechanical, photocopying, recording or otherwise without the written permission of the author.

Published by

Emerge Publishing Group, LLC
Riviera Beach, FL
www.emergepublishers.com

Addie L. Greene 2018
From the Coal Mines to the Board Room

Printed in the United States of America

Contents

Foreword i
Acknowledgements iii
The Prologue v
Chapter 1: Life of a Coal Miner's Family 1
Chapter 2: Currency: Scrip or Clacker 5
Chapter 3: Big Mary's 9
Chapter 4: Finally a Home 15
Chapter 5: Alabama by Product 21
Chapter 6: Stillman College 23
Chapter 7: Some of the Glades First
African American Teachers 33
Chapter 8: Welcome to Palm Beach County 39
Chapter 9: Lake Shore High School 43
Chapter 10: Chiefland High School 47
Chapter 11: Option 2: Desegregation of
Palm Beach County Schools 51
Chapter 12: Police and Politics 61
Chapter 13: Burial of Mrs. Ella Bell Colbert 67
Chapter 14: Redistricting in Palm Beach County 69
Chapter 15: Welcome to the Florida House 73
Chapter 16: Swearing in Ceremony 77
Chapter 17: Mrs. Janice Stanley 79
Chapter 18: District Offices 81
Chapter 19: Portrait of the Black Caucus 85
Chapter 20: The Rosewood Massacre 89

Contents (cont'd)

Chapter 21: One Florida 91
Chapter 22: Why & How a Bill Becomes Law
Remembering Sister Alberta Burden 95
Chapter 23: House Page and Messenger Program 101
Chapter 24: The Palm Beach County Commission 103
Chapter 25: The Beginning of the Palm Beach
County Caucus of the Black Elected Officials 111
Chapter 26: Palm Beach County Caucus of Black
Elected Officials 2013 newly elected
President Terence Davis 121
Chapter 27: Black Caucus in Disarray: Scholarship
Cash in Limbo 123
Chapter 28: Deputies Call for Greene to Resign 127
Chapter 29: Palm Beach County Days 139
Chapter 30: Scripps Research Institute 143
Chapter 31: Blacks, Whites Need Right Leaders 153
Chapter 32: Paragon Florida, Inc. 157
Chapter 33: No One Has to Die from Breast Cancer 159
Chapter 34: Victorious Return to Political Roots 165
About the Author 167
Questions: From the Coal Mines to the Board Room 169
Answers: From the Coal Mines to the Board Room 170

Foreword

People today do not want to be told, but to be shown by living example.

My purpose for writing this book is not new. As African Americans, we have attempted to get our children to read and study their history for years. During black history month, black churches, some public schools, even some businesses plaster on their walls photos of deceased African American heroes and heroines such as Dr. Martin Luther King, Jr., Harriet Tubman, Benjamin Banneker, Frederick Douglas, George Washington Carver, etc. But still teach it as just an exercise in regurgitation and rote memorization.

Students, especially minorities, need to be informed citizens and have an understanding of all levels of government to be able to know how to make a change in the injustices of the system. However, the influence of Face book, Twitter, Google, Linkedin, Youtube, Snapchat, Instagram, etc., has made it difficult to convince them to even pick up a history book. The word "history" to some still connotes "old," "deceased," or "old school."

During my term in the Florida Legislature, the walls of the Chamber of the House of Representatives were being painted. The artist painted on the wall a book about Harry T. Moore entitled *Before His Time* by Ben Green. I asked Representative Anthony Hill, "Who is Harry T. Moore?"

He replied with extreme surprise in his voice, " He was America's first civil rights martyr!"

That was the only black history book I read during my eight years in the Florida legislature. As soon as I left the Florida Legislature and became the County Commissioner, I hosted Mr. Ben Green, the author of *Before His Time* and Ms. Evangeline Moore, the daughter of Harry T. Moore, and students at Suncoast High School to a book signing in the City of Riviera Beach.

As I now look back, I realize I unknowingly used social media to connect students to history. Mr. Ben Green taught history and levels of governmental injustices without the use of social media. He brought Harry T. Moore alive in print during his book signing.

It is now the year 2018, and Palm Beach County has twenty nine black elected officials, more than any county in the state of Florida. It is my hope that this book will help students to understand the significance of their elected officials' service and how it impacts their lives, improves their lack of understanding of all levels of government and the knowledge of their history, the structure of their government, and the names of their elected officials–black and white.

Acknowledgements

It is very difficult to find words to express my true debt of gratitude to the hundreds of people who helped pave the road of my political journey. The works of these individuals resulted in the shaping of this book.

My role model was my mom, the love of my life, who personified courage and strength before she realized her God-given gift of leadership.

My life's journey would be incomplete without the overwhelming support of my 150+ volunteers who never lost hope in our campaign victory!

Fortunately for us, our campaign took place when the political climate in Palm Beach County enabled us to receive support and votes from Democrats, Republicans and friendships such as Dr. Harry Horwich, Bobby Horwich, Dr. Andre Fladell, attorney and former Riviera Beach mayor Michael Brown, former South Bay mayor and friend Clarence Anthony, my loving family and my late best friend, Earlene Jordan-Weston will never be forgotten!

Thanks to the presidents of Palm Beach Junior College, now Palm Beach State College, Dr. Edward Eissey and Dr. Dennis P. Gallon for allowing me to continue to enjoy what I loved most: teaching my students while remaining in the state legislature.

Finally, I respectfully want to acknowledge the photographic talents and contributions of the photographers whose works are included in this book and also Deacons Natalie and Edward Moore of Tabernacle Missionary Baptist Church for hosting the program *Hope from the Hill- 107.1 F.M. Radio Ministry* which helped me launch my book on Facebook and the air waves!

The Prologue

Mothers were the strongest influence in the African American families during the early 40's and 50's due to the obvious divide between the life styles of blacks and whites. In the rural communities of the south, black families lived where the head of the household was employed. When the shortage of workers in northern plants occurred, southern black men in search of better paying jobs boarded trains going north where they found the average income was twice that of the black men in the south. Thus the black women waited and hoped for their return or they succeeded on their own.

That divide was even more prevalent in the coal mines where blacks and whites worked side by side. Every day, as black and white fathers risked their lives, lungs, and limbs working underground in the dark, deep caverns of the earth called coal mines, they prayed their sons' lives would differ from theirs.

They hoped their sons would not have to work in the coal mines and risk dying from black lung, a lung disease that develops from inhaling coal dust.

The name, "black lung," comes from the fact that those with the disease literally have lungs that are black instead of pink. Medically, it is a type of pneumoconiosis called coal workers' pneumoconiosis.

Every family of a coal miner had the same morning schedule. The fathers and mothers awoke at 4:00 a.m. Fathers refreshed the hot coals in the fire place or the heater to warm their three-roomed, wooden-framed shot-gun houses while the mothers prepared breakfast and packed their husband's coal-miner's lunch bucket.

Fathers quickly ate their breakfasts, but not before they kissed their wives as the wives silently prayed that today they would not hear the familiar piercing sound emanating from the coal mines signaling a cave-in. Many families had lost fathers, brothers, and sons, but the loss always felt the same throughout the communities, no matter whose family was chosen that day.

Mom watched Dad leap into the back of the pick-up truck, which held five coal miners; two whites and three blacks. However, when they arrived home in the evening, you only saw five black men covered with coal dust!

We piled on our sweaters and jackets and joined our neighborhood classmates shivering in the cold weather waiting on our over-crowded school bus. Once we entered the bus, our driver, Mr. Johnson always greeted us with a warm smile. Every morning, I looked forward to that warmth to help warm my chilled bodyas he drove us the ten miles one way to Praco High School.

The voices of our teachers and the principal were the most powerful and effective in our school. They wanted us educated the same as whites, but an equal education was impossible due to unequal funding and separate schools, especially those schools located in rural areas such as Black Creek, Alabama.

But God gave us Principal Thomas L. Shaw and teachers such as Mrs. Bethune, Ms. Lois Steele, Mrs. McKinney, Mrs. Brown and our choir directress Mrs. Scott. The faculty did not find it too much to drive seventy five miles round trip so their students received the same or better quality of education as the students at West Jefferson High School.

Every morning, our teachers and our principal began school devotions by leading the student body in the pledge of allegiance to the American flag, the Lord's Prayer, and finally the Negro National Anthem, "Lift Every Voice and Sing," written by James Weldon Johnson.

The housekeeping and general up- keep and heating of the classrooms were supervised by the janitor. Our bathrooms were identical to today's bathrooms, only they were covered out-door structures. There was very little classroom equipment for teachers and students. Three years later, my graduating class of 1961 had twenty seven students.

The school day ended at 4:00 p.m. The big yellow school bus returned to our neighborhood in time for my friend and me to feed the chickens and do our homework. We spent the few hours of sunlight we had left enjoying a bike ride, shooting marbles, playing hop-scotch, or playing on the home-made merry-go-round Dad made from rail-road cross tires or just watching the fire flies before we prepared for the next school day.

At the beginning of our summer vacations, our neighborhoods became family resorts unless our relatives or grandparents lived out of town.

Our mother and her two brothers, Nathaniel and Charlie, never knew their parents. We were told they were murdered when Mom and her brothers were very young, so they were raised by their mother's sister, and her husband, Mr. Henry Boglin. We called them Grandpa and Grandma Boglin. We were just happy that we had someone to visit in Selma, Alabama even if they were our grandparents in name only.

During our summer vacations, my sister Inez and my brother Tom always tried to trick me into babysitting my little brothers Nathaniel and Harry. Inez only wanted to pick vegetables and hang out in the kitchen and cook vegetables with Grandma Boglin.

Even though I loved to eat and read, picking berries and peaches and climbing trees with Tom was more exciting!

The Boglins lived in a large wooden home with large bedrooms that had high ceilings and tin-roofs. The bedroom walls were papered with comic strips to keep out the cold during winter months. My bedroom was one of my favorite places because I could read the comics before I went to bed.

For breakfast every morning, Poppa brought bacon from the smoke house, which was located in the back yard, and fresh eggs still warm from the hen's nest. I couldn't wait for the biscuits and sorghum syrup!

The Prologue

Every house in the community had very large windows on each side, a large white peaked tin roof and a front porch with a swing. Every night I prayed for rain. The soothing sound of rain drops tap, tap, tapping on the tin roof would slowly rock me to sleep.

Making up my bed every morning was easy. I quickly learned to place my hand inside the slit to evenly spread out the cotton balls that were inside the mattress so that no lumps appeared beneath the beautiful handmade quilt, which looked as if someone had hand-painted on it a picture from a magazine.

But no matter how good I felt each morning, I dreaded the daily morning task of emptying the night's bed pan more than I dreaded visiting the outhouse.

The "out-house" was a toilet separate from the house and located in the woods. There was no plumbing, sewer, or septic tank. Much worse, black snakes were drawn to these structures like magnets are drawn to iron. Snakes loved to slither around them, especially when little girls needed to go to the outhouse.

Well, this little girl was never going without her big brother, Tom. He always walked in front of me and held a long stick to fight off the slithering creatures as I hurriedly entered the outhouse, held my nose, and did my business! I don't know which was worse, the horrible smell or my fear of the snakes.

Tom would say over and over, "Hurry up, Atlue. What's taking you so long?"

I never quite finished my business.

During the evening, I enjoyed slowly swinging on the front porch and watching neighbors walk down the long, dark lonely, dusty road, led by kerosene lanterns strategically placed in every window to safely light their way home.

As our summer vacations came to a close, I felt guilty because I never wanted to return to Black Creek. As much as I loved my family, summer vacations at Grandpa and Grandma Boglin's were always packed with enchantment!

At the end of our vacation, we quietly rode home. I kept my eyes glued to the window of our truck until my grandparents became tiny dots and then invisible!

CHAPTER 1

Life of a Coal Miner's Family

One afternoon after school, I heard Dad tell Mom that the government was giving free food to qualified families.

Unfortunately, families of coal miners did not make a lot of money. The little money they earned never made it to their families because they owed their souls to the company commissary.

It did not take Mom long to discover that twice a month, families from the following areas needed transportation to the company warehouse to pick up their commodities and return home: Flat Creek, Wega, Sumiton, Minor, Brookside, Lollar, Hathcock, Chicasaw, Labuco, Goodwin, Gamma Slope, Musgrove, Pratt, and Porter.

Before we knew it, Mom had convinced Dad to allow her to use his pick-up truck to transport the neighbors to the warehouse, and he carpooled with his fellow coal miners. But instead of charging the families, she would accept food instead. Mom became the neighborhood taxicab-driver-for-food!

Before the end of the month, our food pantry looked like a grocery store. Not having to spend money buying food at the store, Mom and Dad saved money toward the building of our home so that we could move out of our shot-gun house.

Several years later, we discovered we were going to get another brother or sister: Mom was six months pregnant! Mom was giving birth so quickly until it seemed she kept her pregnancies a secret.

Mom gave birth to Mack Treadwell, Jr. in 1948. In 1950, Velina, nick named "Bunnie," followed. Mom would stop driving just long enough to give birth and wean her baby before she returned to her job *"driving for commodities."* Our food pantry kept expanding and so did mom's stomach!

Mom always said she wanted to birth a basketball team. Well, she was on her way because in 1951, Deborah became team member seven. Finally, in 1952, Mom decided that she would stop with child number eight, which was a baby girl, Mary, nicknamed Mary Jo.

After our family grew from five siblings to nine, a three roomed shotgun house could not accommodate a family that now totaled eleven. Our summer vacations were now spent helping Mom take care of our three little sisters and baby brother. We desperately needed a larger home.

Our three-room shotgun house was bursting at the seams. But finding a larger house was almost impossible in the rural communities where only shot-gun structured homes existed.

Shot-gun houses were designed in 1810. They were a black cultural architectural form that originated in the American South and were used extensively throughout the region. Shotgun houses were typically long and narrow with a gable ended entrance, one room wide, and two or three rooms deep.

Some say the shotgun house was named because one could fire a shotgun through the front door and the shot would exit out the back door without ever touching a wall. Shotgun houses are still found in many cities and towns in Alabama and throughout the South. They are found in both rural and urban southern areas, mainly in African American communities and neighborhoods. Many are still in use today, and some have been restored to a level of splendor that did not exist when they were first built.

But one day, the entire neighborhood got good news. The coal miner's employer, Alabama by Product, was relocating its workers to a bigger and better coal mining town called Praco Hill. Rumor spread that a larger coal mine meant better pay, more food on the table and larger houses. Finally, Inez and I would have our own room, I assumed.

It took our family of ELEVEN only a day to move from a three room shotgun house to a six room shotgun house. Three rooms faced east and three faced west, but there was a minor difference: the six rooms were longer and wider. But who's looking a gift horse in the mouth? The good part was that the yard was larger and had more dirt. But the house still had no bathroom or indoor plumbing.

The company purchased affordable housing for the families of the miners, but as we discovered, the houses were always in remote areas with no amenities for the children. The miners had to have a place to live and in a very calculated way: the houses kept the workforce beholden to the company. At forty dollars a month, the houses were not built for long term use, but they were adequate for their purpose.

See Gregory Gaynes, New York Times 1981

CHAPTER 2

Currency: Scrip or Clacker

The mining company paid the coal miners for all the tons of coal they mined. The coal miners worked long hours for five or six nights a week. During the 1900s scrips was the credit cards for miners. The miners, mostly from Flat Creek, Palos, Dolomite, Dora and the surrounding areas, were issued a temporary currency called "scrip" or "clacker." This was company money (a substitute for government-issued legal tender or currency), issued by a company to pay its employees. It could only be exchanged in company stores owned by the employers.

Coal miners were paid with coal scrip or tokens or paper with a monetary value issued to workers as an advance on wages by the coal company or its designated representative. Coal scrip could only be used at the specific locality or coal towns the company named.

Because coal scrip was used in the midst of a coal town, where there was usually no other retail establishments, employees who used this form of currency could only redeem value at that specific location. With no other retail establishments, this constituted a monopoly.

The country musician, Merle Travis made a reference to coal scrip in the song, "Sixteen Tons," on the *Folk Songs of the Hills* album. The practice has also been documented as recently as September 2008.

On September 4, 2008, the Mexican Supreme Court of Justice ruled that Wal-Mart de Mexico, the Mexico subsidiary of Wal-Mart, must cease paying employees in part with vouchers redeemable only at Wal-Mart stores.

Workers who were paid in scrip had little choice but to purchase goods at a company store. If the script was exchanged into currency, it would exhaust some of the value because of the exchange fee.

With this economic monopoly, the employer could place large markups on goods, making workers dependent on the company, thus enforcing employee loyalty.

According to the Wisconsin Historical museum, forest products and lumber companies were specifically exempted between 1878 -1890 from the state law that required employers to pay workers' wages in cash. Lumber and timber companies frequently paid their workers in scrip that was redeemable at the company store. Company-run stores served as a *convenience* for workers and their families, but they also allowed the companies to recapture some of their labor expenses. In certain cases, employers included contract provisions requiring employees to patronize the company stores. Employees who wanted to change from scrip to cash generally had to do so at a discount. Lumber company scrip was redeemable in lumber as well as other merchandise.

According to the Wisconsin Historical Society, such an option may have appealed to new settlers in the region, who worked in the lumber camps in the winter to earn enough money to establish a farm. Taking some of their wages in lumber may have helped them build a much needed house or barn.

Sample of clacker currency

Usually coal miners spent the "clacker" at their company store, buying only the limited goods that cost the same as those sold by town merchants. Large companies also issued their own currency to their workers who needed to buy goods between paydays. These companies issued scrip, which was temporary paper currency doled out in books of tear-out-coupons. Clacker, on the other hand, was temporary metal currency that was issued to miners at their request and charged against their earnings.

"Clacker" became more popular in the area than scrip and remained in use until the 60s. The rent for company housing and the cost of items from the company store were deducted from miners' pay. The stores themselves charged inflated prices, since there was no alternative for purchasing goods.

In the 1950s,' states passed laws requiring companies to pay US currency each month. But the defiant coal companies sidestepped these laws by paying in scrip on a weekly or biweekly basis and then paying in cash at the end of each month. This in effect left the miners where they were before the laws were enacted.

According to the *Coal Mines Scrip* by John Freddie Wilson, many states in the 50s' outlawed the use of scrips entirely, and eventually this illegitimate form of currency disappeared from use all together.

The coal industry in Alabama was segregated. From the end of the nineteenth century to the 1930s, approximately one half of all coal miners in Alabama and blacks were more than 90 percent of convicted miners. The 1890 U.S. Census indicates that African Americans made up 46.2 percent of the mining population. Native-born white miners comprised 34.9 percent and 18.7 percent consisted primarily of Southern and Eastern European immigrants. Four decades later, the proportion of black miners expanded to 53.2 percent, native born whites increased to 45.3 percent, and immigrants decreased to 1.5 percent, as the waves of immigration that characterized the turn of the century came to an end.

As a rule, segregation among miners existed above ground because companies provided separate neighborhoods for the different groups. When underground, however, miners earned equal pay for equal work and endured the same hazards and risks of a dangerous occupation. Still, owners and operators often used racial and ethnic differences to pit one group of miners against another in an effort to keep them from organizing.

James Sanders Day. University of Montevallo/Encyclopedia of Alabama

CHAPTER 3

Big Mary's

Mom

Mom constantly complained about how some acted as if life was comfortable living on Praco Hill. If heads of households continued to do nothing about the company padding the miners' ticket at the commissary and denying fathers' their wages for the amount of coal they hauled every day, they would never be able to afford a better life for their families.

As a child, I too was among those who became comfortable living on Praco Hill until I discovered the added miles we now lived from our school. The mining company had no control over the transportation of the children of its employees. Unfortunately, we found ourselves walking ten miles round-trip to school.

Because I wanted to take a typing class, my parents sacrificed to purchase me a Remington typewriter. Imagine trying to walk to school with the extra load of books, band instruments, and a typewriter.

The only family larger than nine children was the Hawkins' family. Finally, Mom and Dad were forced to purchase a used station wagon for our safe transportation to and from school and for our after school activities.

After several months, we arrived home one day after school and heard the voice of Fats Domino singing the song "Blueberry Hill." Never having heard music coming from our house before, we were curious as to its origin.

As we entered the house, we discovered it was coming from a pretty red and white Rock-Ola/Juke *box* sitting against the wall of what used to be our parent's bedroom.

Also, where our parents' chifforobe once was there now appeared a piano. As a matter of fact, as we stared in amazement, we finally realized there was no furniture at all on this side of the house!

As we began to examine the rest of the house, we realized the furniture had been relocated to the opposite side of the house. Where my sisters' bunk beds once sat, there were now red and white tables and chairs accented by red and white curtains that covered the windows. The entrance to the kitchen was no longer accessible to the public. The kitchen door now was blocked by a cross-bar that could only be raised by mom or dad.

Yes, Mom did it again! She discovered another way to supplement Dad's coal miner's salary. She turned our shotgun house into a juke joint! She had even hired a gentleman named Mr. Joe as her guitar player and another man named Monroe Johnson, as her piano player.

When no one dropped coins into the Rock-Ola, Mr. Joe and Monroe "stumped" the down-home blues by black artists such as Bobby Blue Bland, Sam Cooke, Little Richard, and Fats Domino, all night long..

Within a month, the east side of our house became crowded with happy paying customers who enjoyed home brew, chicken and ribs, pickled pig feet, moon shine, fried fish, poker on the front porch or outside in the dark, and anything that made them happy, as long as there was no fighting.

Hard working people came to relax without having to get dressed up to do it. Women came to let their hair down and to enjoy a few drinks and, some good, loud music, and to juke from Friday night until early Sunday morning.

The music became a form of dialogue between black people that made their hearts happy and caused their feet to move, and no one cared about anything else.

Tom, our brother, discovered a funny and private way for all of us, except our three little sisters, to also have fun. He bored a hole through the wall of the closet in our parents' bedroom. Every Friday night through Sunday morning, we enjoyed our private "peep show," watching the adults dance, grind, and act silly when they had too much to drink.

If someone became rowdy or acted as if they wanted to start a brawl, Dad would quickly remind them of the rules of the house: "No fighting and no cursing!"

Dad, a six footer and over 180 pounds, smoked but did not drink. He was Mom's bouncer. His job was always easy because coal miners, black and white, had a special bond and trust for each other.

That trust was tried and tested daily when these same men locked their lamps onto their hats before joining together and entering the earth to face unpredictable gas explosions underground.

Mom and Dad did not want their place to get the reputation that would cause law enforcement to shut them down. Their establishment was the only one allowed to publicly sell alcohol within thirty five miles from the largest city, Birmingham. Their customers knew their only place of entertainment was owned by Big Mary.

Opening a Juke Joint was really not Mom's idea. Ms. Bessie was the first to open her juke joint, but she was not allowed to sell alcohol to her customers. Her customers had to sneak in their alcoholic beverages and be sneaky to drink them.

However, when Mom opened her juke joint, her customers openly drank alcoholic beverages. Mom and Dad provided them on the premises, just as you did in a licensed public bar, only Mom was unlicensed.

As I got older, I learned that Dad and the sheriff, Mr. Pate, were very good friends. Dad also knew the names of the Grand Dragon and some members of the Ku Klux Klan. I quickly learned why I only saw Dad greeting white men at the back kitchen door. They collected their fee and allowed Mom to sell her alcoholic beverages.

During the 50's, juke joints were like bars and nightclubs today. In the late nineteenth century, these establishments catered to the rural work force that began to emerge after the Emancipation. Juke joints were located in the African-American communities because black workers were barred from white establishments in rural Alabama.

The juke joints became household words not only in the surrounding towns, but even in larger cities. Unfortunately, they also became known to law enforcement, which, according to rumors, was also the Ku Klux Klan.

During the 50's one week night after dinner, Mom and Dad were enjoying the swing on the front porch. Suddenly, the honking of car horns surprised all of us. Out of nowhere, bright car headlights appeared slowly meandering through the neighborhood. The bright lights lit up the sky. The light inside of each car enabled us to see the white faces of men wearing white robes with pointed hoods.

This was a familiar sight for Mom and Dad, but it was unfamiliar to our brothers who were playing in the yard. Immediately, Mom began calling our brothers into the house. Inez and I ushered our little sisters away from the windows as Dad closed the curtains! Curiosity forced us to run to the window to watch glaring headlights and listen to the continued honking of the car horns as the cars disappeared into the night.

Finally, instead of seeing bright headlights, we now stared at red taillights and the backs of white hoods. They exited the same way they entered. For a few minutes, we remained still and quiet as Dad closed the curtains. Very calmly, Dad said, *"The KKK."*

After a few more months and a few more parades of this kind, the neighborhood children and adults became tolerant of these bold displays of racism. The Ku Klux Klan believed the crosses they burned in our neighborhoods frightened us and kept us subservient, afraid and controlled. They soon discovered that was not always the case.

The Klan always selected only one church to burn its cross on its lawn: the Church of God in Christ, (COGIC). As kids, we called this church the sanctified church.

CHAPTER 4

Finally a Home

Because Mom and her two brothers were not raised by their real parents, Mom's philosophy became Families that pray together, stay together.

Since Inez was attending college, Bunnie, Debra, and Mary became my responsibility, especially during the weekends.

Dad and Mom devised a way to check on us while they worked and took care of their customers. They each took turns and brought such treats as cake, ice cream, chicken wings, pickled pig feet, boiled eggs, pickles, or fried fish. With four growing boys, the food was never wasted. This made us look forward to the weekends.

Tom and I suddenly realized that the more extra time Mom and Dad had to make money, the sooner we would be able to move into a home that we owned. As I braided my three sisters' hair in preparation for school every day, I remembered Mom's words to me: "Atlue, soon we will be able to move into our own house. Then you will have your own room."

I was fourteen years old when that day finally arrived! Only this time, it took us less time and trouble to move into our new home than it took to move into the shot-gun house. Once there, I discovered a completely furnished home of nine rooms and a huge basement. Not only had Dad and his brother, Uncle Zedic been building the home, but they had been furnishing it at the same time. That was when I realized we had brought very little furniture with us.

We were the first black family to move from the town of Praco Hill into our home in West Jefferson. The small town had only one traffic light. A fact that still remains true.

There were large, beautiful brick and wooden houses, green lawns, mail boxes, large trees, a grocery store, a post office, and two bridges. One of the bridges just happened to be located in front of our home.

No more out-houses or black snakes! Most of all, Mom could finally become a stay-at-home-mom and enjoy the home she always wanted! Only one thing was missing: people that looked like us.

Our Family Home

After we settled into our home, Dad and Mom assumed the Ku Klux Klan had learned that their racial tactics had become ineffective in frightening black folks. But they were wrong.

One night or early morning, the KKK sneaked into the neighborhood and left our family a warning! We were awakened by a blast of a bomb so loud that it shook the walls of our home! This time it was a Molotov cocktail instead of a parade of cars. Surprisingly, Dad quieted the family and we all went to our rooms, of course, no one slept.

The following morning, we watched as Dad joined his black and white fellow coal miners on the back of the pickup truck. When he returned home from work, he went directly to shower the black coal dust from his body and then joined the family for dinner. Our anticipation was overpowering as we patiently waited to hear him tell us of his fellow miners' reactions.

We were disappointed when Dad told us there was no mention of the bomb. That was our final experience with Molotov cocktails and men in white pointed robes.

Voices and laughter of eight children instead of nine filled our new home because Inez was now attending college. Returning home from school and smelling Mom's home cooking throughout our home eased the painful and unforgettable memories of the outdoor bathrooms and the inconveniences and sacrifices our family had endured for years.

However, soon Mom's baby girl, Mary, became a first grader. Mom was home alone, and we were getting our high-school education during the day while Dad toiled in the coalmines.

Mom, still weighing less than 150 pounds and standing only five feet, who would have imagined she would take the test to become a school bus driver for the Jefferson County public school system? Amazingly, she became the driver of one of the longest buses on the yard. However, only four of her children, Mack, Velina, Debra, and Mary, rode to school with Mom, while my three brothers and I drove. Mom and Dad retired once the girls were in college.

Every little town that made up her routes was located in the woods, on a hill, down a hill, around a dead curve, or under a hanging bridge. The area was so scary that she and Dad continued to allow Tom to drive us to school until we all graduated. Therefore, after we moved from Praco Hill, to West Jefferson, we never rode a school bus.

Tom and I graduated from Praco High School in 1961, and I enrolled in Stillman College in Tuscaloosa, Alabama. Tom entered the coal mines and married Bobby Nell Harris. They had two children, Jerome and Denise. Mack Treadwell, Jr. graduated from high school, entered Daniel Payne Junior College, but he was drafted into the army for the Vietnam War, where he served and received a Purple Heart. After two years, he returned home, became a coal miner, married his sweet heart, Lillian Tart, and built her a home in West Jefferson before the birth of their two children, Myra and Mack Treadwell III. Nathaniel Green, graduated from high school and took his bride Geraldine Reynolds, with him to live in Detroit, where he opened his own janitorial service, built a home, and raised their daughter, Kimberly, and granddaughter, Madison.

West Jefferson High School was within walking distance of our home, so my baby sister Mary Jo eventually became a West Jefferson High School senior. Before she graduated from West Jefferson, she competed for Miss West Jefferson High and won fourth place. She graduated and entered Alabama A&M University in Huntsville, Alabama and earned her Bachelor's Degree.

**(Standing) James Harper, Jr., Marbris Dillard, Inez Johnson-Treadwell, John A. Willis
(Sitting) Debra Treadwell-Carmichael, Addie L. Greene, Mary Treadwell-Gray,
Velina Treadwell-O'Neal**

Kimberly now resides in Atlanta, Georgia with her daughter Madison. Nathaniel now works as a paralegal.

Top Row - L to R: Phyllis & Jerrisa Green, Antony , Harry & Harold Green, John Willis, Donzell Treadwell, Addie Greene
Second Row - L to R: Debra Carmichael, Vicky Green , Velina Treadwell, Mary Gray
Children - L to R: Antonio Green, Jr., Jerell Green, Justin Green, Jasmine Green,

CHAPTER 5

Alabama by Product

Dad and some of his fellow coal miners received their pens for ten years of service and were photographed with the superintendent of Generating Company, a mine owned by Alabama by Product.

Back Row: Dad, second left, with his fellow coalminers

Harry Greene served in the army, returned home and married Celia Mae Johnson. Celia gave birth to Tony Green and twin sons, Harold and Harry Green, who now live in Florence, Alabama.

Velina Treadwell graduated from Tuskegee University and married John Willis, Sr. Velina and John had a son, John Willis, Jr. Velina retired from teaching and now resides in Grand Prairie, Texas with her son, his wife and their two children, Nichols and Jahni Willis.

Mary Treadwell Gray graduated from Alabama A & M University and married J. C. Gray. After a successful career, she retired from teaching and continues to live in Palm Beach County.

After Debra Treadwell graduated from nursing school, she married and gave birth to Marbris Dillard and Donzell Treadwell. After her divorce, she and her sons relocated to Palm Beach County, where she married Harvey Carmichael. She too had a successful career in her chosen field of nursing before ultimately retiring.

Inez attended Daniel Payne Junior College, and from there, she enrolled in nursing school. Eventually, she moved to Detroit, Michigan, and married Milton Johnson, now deceased. Inez has three children: Thoris, Cathy, and Milton Johnson Jr. She retired and lives with her daughters in Bowie, Maryland.

CHAPTER 6

Stillman College

Two of my favorite teachers, my English teacher, Ms. Lois Steele and my guidance counselor, Mrs. McKinney, were the reasons I narrowed my college choices to attend one of the two historical black colleges: Stillman College in Tuscaloosa, Alabama or Wilberforce University in Wilberforce, Ohio.

I was accepted to both schools, but Wilberforce was my first choice. The Stillman scholarship came with the requirement that after graduation, I had to teach in a migrant area or I would have to repay the money.

I didn't have an issue with teaching in a migrant area; I just wanted to get as far away from Alabama as the Grey hound bus could take me! Unfortunately, my parents decided I was too inexperienced (their way of saying too country) to live that far from home, especially for four years. So Stillman College was destined to be my home for the next four years.

The excitement of finally leaving home the next morning kept me awake. Curiosity about college campus life had overwhelmed me since Inez left home. Before I went to sleep, Mom entered my room with a husky, black male doll wearing only a diaper. With a smile on her face, she placed it on my bed and said, "Atlue, Mom wants this to be the only male in your bed!"

Embarrassed, I thought to myself, "Only my mother would send me to college with a black doll baby!" Then I remembered. When she and Dad took Inez to Daniel Payne Community College, Mom returned talking about seeing girls carrying teddy bears and dolls into their dormitories. I guess this was Mom's way of making sure I did not get pregnant. She had never been the type of mom to have the "birds and the bees" conversation, but nevertheless, she got her point across.

Well, that was in 1961. Today, as I write this book, that doll is fifty-one years old and sits in a rocking chair in my living room wearing a white shirt with a matching plaid bow tie and cummerbund and green pants held up with matching suspenders.

As we drove to Stillman College the next day, I sat in the back seat and wondered what college life would have been like at Wilberforce University.

When we arrived at Stillman, student volunteers directed us to Winsborough Hall, the freshman and sophomore dormitory for women. As Mom and Dad signed in, the receptionist requested my identification papers. Then she spoke directly to Dad because males were never allowed in the rooms of females, except to help with luggage or an emergency.

"Mr. Treadwell, you are welcome to help settle your daughter into her room. But you must return to the lobby and wait for Mrs. Treadwell."

At that moment, Mom's face lit up like a Christmas tree. I read her mind. "No men allowed in the girls' rooms!"

My roommate, Elizabeth Arrington, arrived a day early. After introductions, Dad returned to the lobby to wait for Mom to complete her interrogation of my roommate. Finally, Mom knew my roommate was an only girl with four brothers and she was the first in her family to attend college. Most of all, Mom was glad to discover Elizabeth's father was a minister and her mother a teacher.

As soon as possible, Mom and I rejoined Dad in the lobby. As I walked them to the car, I realized at that moment that I was sad and afraid for them to leave. As I watched them drive away, I knew I would not disappoint them.

Elizabeth and I spent the weekend learning the campus and making new friends. Early Monday morning, we were among the first to enter Birthright Auditorium for freshman orientation.

During the faculty introductions, I was shocked to learn that our college president, Dr. Samuel N. Hay, was a white man. White administrators and white teachers teaching black students! This was a first for me.

After orientation, we rushed to registration. Only this time, we stood in line for over an hour. Following registration, we returned to our rooms and compared our schedules. I was the one who would need to set her alarm clock for 6:00 a.m. every Tuesday and Thursday to report to cafeteria duty at 7:30 a.m.

Monday morning, we prepared to attend our first class, which was French at 8:00 a.m. It was a Monday, Wednesday and Friday class. Elizabeth arrived early and saved me a seat next to her on the front row. When I entered the classroom, students were laughing and speaking to each other, but in a language I didn't comprehend. I looked at my schedule to make sure I had entered the right class. Suddenly, I heard Elizabeth call my name.

"Hey, Addie, venez vous asseoir ici. Nous vous economise un siege."

It was Elizabeth. But was she speaking to me? She pointed to the seat next to her. I nervously took my seat. The instructor stood in front of the class and began to speak in French. I remained silent and watched Elizabeth as she smiled and shook her head while listening to the instructor.

The instructor's mouth moved, but my mind flashed back to the voice of my English teacher, Ms. Lois Steele. "It is better to remain silent and be thought ignorant, than to open your mouth and remove all doubt."

Immediately after class, I ran, not walked, to the registration office, asked for my first withdrawal form and changed my major from French to English and my minor to business education. It did not take me long to realize conversations in French were easy in my high school because I learned only the basics. The students in this class were born and raised in the cities and towns where their everyday conversations were spoken in French.

The following Tuesday morning, I reported to the cafeteria at 7:15 a.m. to discover my job title was "dishwasher." During my freshman year, my dish washing job and my studying left little time for extracurricular activities. When allowed, I sometimes found time to socialize in the Tiger's Den, where Stillmanites gathered every night from 7:00 p.m. to 10:00 p.m. except on Sundays.

Finally, at the end of my freshman year, I enjoyed free time with my friends and roommate. One night in 1962, Stillmanites filled the Tiger's Den. I entered, but students were not dancing, and there was no sound of music. The den room was quiet. All eyes were on the television. The students listened and stared at the man on the television screen. I waited patiently for a few more minutes and finally asked, "Who is he?"

A male voice from among the crowd sounded, "He's the president of the United States!"

All eyes were now on me. Suddenly, the room was quiet. Embarrassment overwhelmed me. At that moment, a dark cloud covered me and made me think about such a question coming from a college student!

This caused a complete change in my life as I continued to seek my college degree. At that embarrassing time in my college life I began to become more aware of occurrences on campus and the tumultuous state of Alabama and especially Tuscaloosa. Soon I joined many Stillmanites who were becoming involved in the civil unrest that was happening nationally as well as on our campus.

In 1962, I joined the Tuscaloosa Citizens for Action Committee (TCAC), which was a self-defense group that desegregated downtown lunch counters and city buses. In May of that year, we joined the bus boycott, and each of us sat on the front seat of the bus and refused to move to the back of the city bus. All buses and institutions in Tuscaloosa were segregated at that time, in spite of the bus desegregation laws that came about after the bus boycotts spurred by Rosa Parks and Dr. King in 1955. This bus boycott led by TCAC successfully integrated the buses in Tuscaloosa.

On the heels of the integration of the city buses in Tuscaloosa, came Alabama Governor George Wallace's infamous stand in the schoolhouse door at the University of Alabama on June 11, 1963.

George Wallace, the Democratic governor of Alabama, in a symbolic attempt to keep his inaugural promise of segregation now, segregation tomorrow, segregation forever was determined to stop the desegregation of schools. He stood at the door of the Foster Auditorium to block the entry of two black students, Vivian Malone and James Hood. This incident brought Wallace into the national spotlight.

Vivian Malone entering Foster Auditorium to register for classes at the University of Alabama.

Governor Wallace stands in the auditorium door to prevent the integration of the University of Alabama in 1963.

Before the death of Ms. Vivian Malone in 2005 from complications following a stroke, she stated, "I would be remiss and indeed wrong if I did not point to those close at hand, certainly my family but also all the people of the Tuscaloosa community who rallied to my side. I could not have done what I did without Stillman College and the people on Tuscaloosa's West End. They provided my safe haven. And I often think of what they did for Autherine Lucy. That brave and courageous woman first opened the door of this university in 1956 only to have it slammed in her face by a howling mob that the university did not, perhaps could not, stand up to. She fled to safety in the same community that would put its arms around me."

June 9, 1964, was known as "Bloodied Tuesday" in Tuscaloosa because on that day a lot of black blood was shed in the streets of Tuscaloosa in the fight for civil rights. On that day, Stillman College students took part in an attempt to integrate the newly constructed Tuscaloosa County Courthouse.

At that time, we frequently used the First African American Baptist Church on Stillman Boulevard for meetings and planning. On this particular day, the church was attacked and canisters of tear gas were thrown through the windows. Women were beaten with billy clubs while trying to escape by jumping out a window at the church.

A person by the name of Willy Wales, along with her brother, and a number of other college students from Stillman and I tried to escape through a rear window of the church. We were arrested in front of what is now the Murphy African American Museum. Some of us were arrested as we attempted to make it to the courthouse.

One person found refuge in a church closet. While hiding in the closet, she mixed every chemical she found available and threw the mixture in the face of the first person who opened the closet door. Tragically, he was a citizen involved in the demonstration who meant to rescue and not to harm; however, the chemicals seriously burned his eyes. I never did learn what happened to him or the woman who threw the mixture.

During this same time, Stillman college students, faculty and staff hid some of the civil rights fighters who sought refuge in different dormitories on our campus. One building was Snedecor Hall, which at one point housed the Nurses' Training School and hospital. Snedecor was one of the only places in this part of the state where African Americans obtained healthcare.

Ms. Joan Baez was one of the most popular folk singers during these demonstrations. She was also known for promoting social justice, civil rights, and pacifism. On one of her visits to Stillman College, our Westminster Gospel Chorus accompanied her as she sang "All My Trials" and "We Shall Overcome." Ms. Baez was also invited to sing, "We Shall Overcome" at the March on Washington in 1963, which was organized by Dr. Martin Luther King, Jr.

Addie Greene & Joan Baez at Stillman College

As a membr of the Westminster Gospel Chorus, I began a friendship with Ms. Baez during her short stay on our campus. We maintained that friendship until my last letter from her in 1985.

CHAPTER 7

Some of the Glades First African American Teachers

Most of the very first black teachers in the Glades never lost their love for the Glades or its people. They continued to be staunch advocates for the community, especially during the perilous, financial and moral times!"

Daniel Bythwood
Everglades High 1953

Eddie Queen Blakely
Lake Shore High 1964

Gerald Burke
Lake Shore High 1958

Kevin Boynton
Pahokee High 1975

Juanita Daphine
Everglades Voc. 1952

Hodges Davis
East Lake High 1951

Mildred Fernandez
East Lake High 1959

Rubin Finley
East Lake High 1959

Emanuel Garrett
Pahokee High 1959

Mary Gray
Pahokee Elementary 1987

Addie L. Greene
Pahokee High 1967

Doris D. Harrell
East Lake High 1967

Freddie Jefferson
Lake Shore High 1957

John Jenkins
Lake Shore High 1955

Geraldine Johnson
East Lake High 1969

Some of the First Glades First African American Teachers

James Johnson
East Lake High 1957

Daisy B. Lanier
East Lake High 1958

Jackie Morrison
Lake Shore Elem. 1953

Julia Anita Scott
East Lake Elem. 1959

Willie Singletary
Lake Shore High 1957

Getchrell Singleton
South Bay High 1951

John H. Stephens
Lake Shore Elem. 1961

Velina Treadwell
Lake Shore Middle 1974

Glades Teachers Listed Below Without Photos

NAME	YEAR	SCHOOL
Ernest Anderson		
Geraldine Anderson		
Geraldine Atkins	1979	Pahokee High
Francine Baines	1965	
Agnes Balfour=		
Joseph Bell		
Myrtis Burke		
Ruby Butts		Grove Elementary
Lillian Cambridge		
Edith Coleman		
Betty Collier		
Fannie Cousin		
Gwendolyn Davis	1969	Pahokee High
Mildred Dupont		
Muriel Evans		
Mildred Fernandez	1964	East Lake High
Edward Fitzgerald		
Mary Jane Ford	1969	
Julia Fountain		
Patricia Fretwell		
Irene Gibson		
Dr. Effie Grear		Glades Central
Emma Hall		

Some of the First Glades First African American Teachers

NAME	YEAR	SCHOOL
Freddie Harrell	1970	Pahokee High
Louis Henderson		
Ida R.R.L. Irvin		
James "Jeff" Jefferson	1950	Lake Shore High
Jessie Jenkins	1962	Lake Shore High
Benjamin Johnson	1970	Pahokee High
Dorothy Johnson	1969	Pahokee High
Mae Ida Keys		
Barbara Kight		
Arthur King	1970	
Hazel Poole Kinsey	1964	East Lake High
Dr. Barbara Madison	1969	Pahokee High
Patricia Manor		
Hanna Means	1969	Pahokee High
Ashton Miller	1969	Pahokee High
Joseph Morris	1969	Pahokee High
Betty Collier Murray		
Louise Murray		
Wilhelmina Pittman	1970	Pahokee High
Estelle Pyfrom	1971	Pahokee High
Willie Pyfrom		Belle Glade High
Mae Ross		Rosenwald Elementary
Antoine Russell	1969	Pahokee High
Geraldine Russell		
Rachael Sarvise		

NAME	YEAR	SCHOOL
James "Jeff" Jefferson	1950	Lake Shore High
Julia Anita Scott	1959	East Lake Elementary
Hattie Singletary		
Julia Stephens		
Betty Thompson	1969	Pahokee High
Ernest Thompson	1969	East Lake/Pahokee High
Julia Thompson	1969	Pahokee High
Willie James Thompson		
Hoover Tolbert		
Oris Walker		
Willie U. Walker		
Mary Washington		
Shirley Weaver		
Willie Mae White		
Dorothy Williams	1969	Pahokee High
Patricia Williams		
Ida Wilson		
Marian Wilson	1985	
Elease Young		

CHAPTER 8

Welcome to Palm Beach County

As I boarded the Greyhound bus in Birmingham and sat in the front seat behind the bus driver, I vowed this would be my last ride on another Greyhound. Once we boarded and took our seats, the bus driver announced, "Welcome aboard ladies and gentlemen."

During the sixties, most buses stopped to pick up everywhere except cornfields, so I knew I was in for a long bus ride. However, once we crossed the Alabama and Georgia state line, college graduates leaving home to seek employment gradually began to fill the back of the bus. There were many sorority, fraternity, basketball and football sweaters. Regrettably, I now wished for the back of the bus! The atmosphere became friendlier as students became acquainted and shared addresses.

Once we entered Florida, the bus driver began his announcements: "Ladies and gentlemen, we are approaching Tallahassee" or "Ladies and gentlemen, we are approaching Jacksonville, Gainesville, Daytona, Orlando, and Fort Pierce." It seemed I would never hear him say West Palm Beach.

Soon, the words, "Good luck," "Glad to meet you," or "I will call you," became the norm as students and passengers exited the bus. It seemed we rode another thousand miles before I finally heard, "Ladies and gentlemen, our next stop is West Palm Beach!" Now I was the last college student on the bus.

"The Helen Wilkes Hotel" was the first writing I saw, and then, like magic, I finally saw the letters "West Palm Beach Greyhound Bus Station." Passengers stood and began gathering personal belongings. As I stood, the bus driver said to me, "Young lady, this is not your stop."

"But my ticket says West Palm Beach," I said quietly.

"You are in West Palm Beach, but you get off in Belle Glade," he answered with a smile.

Embarrassed, confused, and trembling, I stumbled back to my seat, too afraid and too embarrassed to speak.

The bus slowly rolled away from the hotel and the bus station. As I shook, I was glad I sat alone! The bus continued to roll slowly past the beautiful glare of bright lights and shiny buildings into the dark shadows of the night until there were no bright lights or traffic lights. We rode for what seemed like hours in complete darkness. The only other vehicles on the roads were large buses, but they did not appear to be Greyhound buses!

As the sun began to rise, I saw rows and rows of sugar cane. I began to talk and to pray to God. I asked God to save me. From what, I didn't know. My family didn't know where I was. I didn't know where I was! My ticket said West Palm Beach, but I wouldn't be able to tell Mom where I was because the bus driver left West Palm Beach for a city called Belle Glade.

Suddenly, I realized I was the only student on the bus. My mind became filled with images of black snakes, outdoor toilets, and white men in white hooded robes.

After riding for several more hours, I saw men and women dressed as if they were going to pick cotton. I thought to myself, "I didn't know they picked cotton in Florida."

Suddenly, the bus driver announced, "Ladies and gentlemen, your destination, Belle Glade."

He stopped the bus in front of a tiny building with the Greyhound logo painted on its side. Once he opened the doors, I tried standing, but my legs wobbled from sitting so long. The driver politely took hold of my hand. As soon as I felt the earth beneath my feet, I heard a voice say, "Are you Ms. Addie Greene?" He knew my name, but I didn't know him.

He realized I had not moved, so he stepped toward me. "I am Principal Charles McCurdy," he said as he reached me and shook my hand. Trying to appear confident, I said, "Yes, I am."

"Your parents told me when you were arriving," he said. "I am the principal of Lake Shore High School. I am here to take you to the home of Mr. and Mrs. Colbert."

Once I was inside his vehicle, he began to tell me about the housing shortage for teachers. He arranged for me to live with Mrs. Ella Bell Colbert, one of his cafeteria workers, and her husband, Mr. Ed.

Once we parked in their yard, the front door opened immediately. Standing before me were two people who were opposites: the wife was five feet tall, round, brown, jolly and very bowlegged, while the husband was skinny and very quiet.

They had no children. Both had been born and reared in Georgia and had lived in Belle Glade since the 1928 storm, which was a surprise attack on coastal residents in Belle Glade between September 6 and 20, 1928. The storm hit Florida with winds of 125 miles per hour. For two hours it ripped apart boats and battered homes. But most residents had taken cover, and deaths were few. But forty miles west, rain filled Lake Okeechobee to the rim. Then a wind from the north began pushing tons of lake water to the south. The dike crumbled, and water rushed onto the swampy farmland. Homes and people were swept away. But these two angels were saved from those torrid waters and lived to tell me about it over and over again.

Mr. Ed never spoke unless spoken to and was as quiet as a mouse. On the other hand, Mrs. Bell never stopped talking, cooking, cleaning and praying. I immediately fell in love with them!

CHAPTER 9

Lake Shore High School

It took only a few weeks for me to realize how convenient and blessed my living arrangements were. They had no children and lived by themselves. Mrs. Colbert had never learned to drive an automobile, so her husband drove her everywhere, even to school, which worked out perfectly for me.

My life changed greatly once I met Patricia Williams, who grew up in the beautiful city of Riviera Beach. After her retirement from the classroom, she became a travel specialist for the company called Elite Travel. She now resides in Atlanta, but in all of her travels, she remains an active member of Delta Sigma Theta Sorority. I am a member of Alpha Kappa Alpha Sorority, but she and I never allowed our differences in Greek loyalty to separate our friendship. It didn't take her long to introduce me to the Palm Beach Mall and Palm Beach County, but she could never force me to drive State Road 80, which during the sixties was called "Killer Highway." Therefore, when she and I were teachers at Lake Shore, she was the chauffeur wherever we traveled, because I was not a licensed driver, but that was about to change.

For the first couple of months, Mrs. Colbert and I were chauffeured to school daily by her husband. However, that lasted just long enough for me to receive a couple of pay-checks. After three months, I purchased my dream car, a 1965 green mustang without a drivers' license. The only proof needed was a membership in the Palm Beach County Teacher's Credit

Union. My parents did not believe I purchased a vehicle without a driver's license until they looked out the window and saw I was home for the Christmas holiday!

As I now look back, only God knows how I safely drove to Alabama and returned to Belle Glade to teach and learn a lasting lesson in humility!

One of my students, the principal's son, was named Ronald McCurdy Jr., and my landlady was one of the principal's favorite cafeteria workers. Therefore, the new car and those two qualities made me feel so special and so absorbed in my own ego that I forgot two things:

1. A teacher's best friends are the principal, the cafeteria workers and the janitors.
2. A teacher's future depends on a continuing contract.

During the first couple of months of the school year, the Safety Patrol from an elementary school took its annual visit to Washington, D.C. School Safety Patrol members are school-sponsored student volunteers from upper elementary grades and middle and junior high schools. Patrollers direct children, not traffic. As school-age leaders in traffic safety, patrol members teach other students about traffic safety on a peer-to-peer basis and serve as models for younger children, who look up to them.

Ronald McCurdy, Jr. went along to Washington with the student patrol and returned to my class without an excuse.

During the roll call, I asked for his permission slip. He replied, "I went to Washington with the Safety Patrol. I don't have one."

I replied, "You are not a member of the Safety Patrol. You still have to have a permission slip. Who do you think you are?"

"I am Ronald McCurdy Jr. That's who I am!"

"Well, you can go to the principal's office, and don't return until you have one!"

Of course, at the end of that day, Ronald McCurdy and his teacher Addie L. Greene were in the principal's office.

At the end of a very heated discussion, Principal McCurdy said to me, "Ms. Greene, you asked him who he thought he was, and he told you he was Ronald McCurdy. What did you expect him to say?"

The voices from the principal's office were so loud that the teachers in the lounge heard them. Somewhere in the midst of this meeting, I forgot this man was the principal and my boss, and could fire me.

I responded, "I don't care what his name is. He is not returning to my class without a permission slip!" I stormed out of the principal's office and slammed his door. As I entered the teacher's lounge, their silence foreshadowed my final days at Lake Shore High School. During the summer of 1966, I was not surprised to receive notice that I was not reassigned to teach at Lake Shore.

CHAPTER 10

Chiefland High School

When the school year ended, instead of vacationing with my family, I instead spent the summer in Belle Glade filling out applications for positions as an English teacher wherever there was a vacancy.

At the beginning of the 1966-67 school years God answered my prayers. But not as an English teacher, but instead as an assistant librarian in the Levy County School District, in Chiefland, Florida, at Chiefland High School, grades one through twelve.

Even though the Dewey Decimal System was the only thing I remembered about a library, the telephone call from Principal Guy Germany was all it took to convince me to accept the position. He never specifically said that the position was for an English teacher. Out of desperation, I was afraid and embarrassed I had placed myself into such a situation where all I wanted was a job.

During the 50s' and 60s', housing for teachers or any professional was difficult to find in the state of Florida if you were black. Even though there was a housing shortage for teachers in the Glades, there were communities within driving distance from the Glades where professionals could rent or purchase beautiful homes because Palm Beach County is an affluent county; however, there was no housing for any black professionals in the city of

Chiefland, unless you drove thirty miles to Gainesville, where minorities were not yet accepted in decent neighborhoods.

My landlady was a very nice, robust, motherly woman who welcomed me to rent a room in her rooming house. My age, profession, and sex became my guarantee. Teachers were held in high esteem.

During faculty orientation, I was surprised to discover there were thirty-nine faculty members, but only two were black: a young girl wearing an afro and me.

After faculty introductions, a charming white lady with coal black hair and with a beautiful snow white streak that made her look like she could be anyone's grandmother tapped me on my shoulder and said, "Ms. Greene, my name is Marguerite Renfroe, the librarian. May I show you the library?"

She immediately assumed I was a graduate of Florida A&M University because she had earned her BS and Ed Degrees from the University of Florida. Surprisingly, she knew the exact location of my alma mater, Stillman College. She was the first white person I had ever felt was not "faking her friendship."

After several months of her assistance and the relationships I developed with students, the library no longer was a place of discomfort but of comfort! Looking back, I did not realize the impact the Chiefland High School library would have on my future. As the assistant librarian, I became an avid reader because the information was so accessible. There was not much black history in the library, but there were articles, especially of black and civil unrest!

The Rosewood Massacre took me by surprise, and I could not stop reading about it. My landlady filled in what I did not read. Chiefland High

School Library and the Rosewood Massacre would eventually have an important place in my future.

The Rosewood Massacre was a racially motivated massacre of black people and destruction of a black town that took place during the first week of January 1923 in rural Levy County, Florida. At least six black people and two white people were killed though eyewitness accounts suggested a death toll as high as 150. The town of Rosewood was abandoned and destroyed in what contemporary news reports characterized as a race riot.

Prior to the massacre, the town of Rosewood had been a quiet, primarily black, self-sufficient whistler stop on the Seaboard Air Line Railway. Trouble began when white men from several nearby towns lynched a black Rosewood resident because of unsupported accusations that a white woman in nearby Sumner had been beaten and possibly raped by a black drifter. When the town's black citizens rallied together to defend themselves against further attacks, a mob of several hundred whites combed the countryside hunting for black people, and burned almost every structure in Rosewood. Survivors from the town hid for several days in nearby swamps until they were evacuated by train and car to larger towns.

Although state and local authorities were aware of the violence, no arrests were made for what happened to Rosewood. The town was abandoned by its former black residents; none ever moved back.

Although the rioting was widely reported around the United States at the time, few official records documented the event. Survivors, their descendants and the perpetrators remained silent about Rosewood for decades.

In 1993, as a member of the Florida Legislature, we commissioned a report on the massacre. As a result of the findings, Florida became the first U.S. state to compensate survivors and their descendants for damages incurred because of racial violence.

As Forrest Gump said in the movie *Forrest Gump,* "The world is like a box of chocolates. You never know what you're gonna get!"

At the end of my teaching career at Chiefland High School in 1968, Principal Germany was very helpful with my return to Belle Glade and to a position as an English teacher at East Lake Junior-Senior High School in Pahokee, Florida.

I left Chiefland High School not only with my pride intact, but also with a letter of recommendation from Principal Germany written to Principal Hamilton of East Lake High School. Unfortunately, after I had been teaching for only one year, the desegregation of Palm Beach County schools disrupted my teaching career once again!

CHAPTER 11

Option 2: Desegregation of Palm Beach County Schools

During the summer of 1968, approximately two hundred Pahokee High School students held a peaceful demonstration in front of Pahokee High School to protest the adoption of Option 2, the planned desegregation of Palm Beach County schools by the Palm Beach County School Board. The students were led by George H. Tucker III, president of the student council; Jimmy Wilson, a member of the senior class; and Norman Seabrook, a graduating senior and an all-area football player who was the recipient of an athletic scholarship to the Citadel.

After the rally, the group gathered around the school's flagpole, repeated the pledge of allegiance to the flag and sang the school alma mater. Tucker, the son of City Councilman George H. Tucker, Jr., spoke.

"The parents of the students are the ones to carry the fight to Atlanta and Washington," he said. "We plan to continue our regular attendance at classes and to conduct ourselves in an orderly manner."

The Pahokee School was the first in the county to be integrated four years in a row. Brooks Henderson, the high school principal, said he was proud of the student body that had cooperated to carry out the freedom of-choice plan without a major incident. After the brief demonstration, Principal Henderson called the faculty into the auditorium for briefing sessions. The principal said later that he would know more about the planned change in school operation after a meeting of administration heads.

"I promised the student body I would let them know what the situation is and what is going to happen when they return to school Monday," Mr. Henderson continued. "There will be no classes as a teachers' workshop has been previously scheduled."

"We were the first school in the county to integrate, and we are getting along okay," said Mr. Henderson in an interview with the Palm Beach Post newspaper.

During the same time as the *1968 Option 2* demonstration was occurring by the students of Pahokee High school, the following six black teachers were being transferred from East Lake to Pahokee High School: Assistant Principal Ernest Thompson, Dorothy Williams, Gwendolyn Davis, Julia Thompkins, Barbara Madison and Addie Greene-Lincoln.

During the first faculty meeting, I was introduced to Betty Wadlington, the chair of the English department, and Hugh Brady, the chair of the history Department, who also assigned me to teach Black History.

As an English teacher, my English assignment was anticipated, but the Black History assignment was a total surprise. In college, the only black history book I read was *Before the May Flower* by Lerone Bennet Jr. Again, I felt this was not going to be a very good year!

My classroom text books were provided, so I chose the text book *Before the May Flower* since the title selection was at my discretion!

The first day of class, there were as many black students as whites. Obviously, the white students registered out of curiosity, and the black students out of pride. After roll call, I shared some of my personal civil rights struggles during my college days and compared them to the present.

The entire class came alive with teenage stories, laughter, and opinions. To maintain their interest for the next day, I assigned the chapters about the beautiful and tragic love story between a man and woman named Antoney and Isabella who were stolen from Africa.

After several weeks of discussing the merchandising and marketing of human beings and the "greatest human migration in recorded history," it was now time to test them on what they learned the first six weeks. Fourteen black students out of fifteen passed, but only two whites out of ten passed. Regrettably, by the end of the course, only one white female student remained.

Thankfully, at the end of the semester, black history disappeared from my teaching schedule and was replaced by the drama club as an extracurricular activity. Some extracurricular activities did not require lesson plans. They were treated as a social hour and carried no academic credit: they were not part of the regular schedule of classes and were held every Friday, and therefore, they quickly filled to capacity.

On the first day, the students elected officers: Kathy McConnell, Jewel Everette, Robbie Everette, Debra Boyd, and Rick Lampros. Noticeably, they did everything in twos: a black president, white vice president; a white secretary, a black assistant secretary; etc.

Each Friday, I used weekly magazines to study theatre. One Friday, a magazine featured a short version of the play, *West Side Story*. We studied plot, scenes, and characters. Students soon enjoyed becoming characters.

At the completion of the magazine version, they wanted to read the long version. The following Friday, I introduced them to *West Side Story*, the award-winning adaptation of the classic romantic tragedy, *Romeo and Juliet,* written by William Shakespeare.

The play transformed two feuding families into two warring New York City gangs–the white Jets led by Riff and the Puerto Rican Sharks, led by Bernardo. Their hatred escalated to a point where neither could coexist with any form of understanding. When Tony, Riff's best friend and a former Jet met Bernardo's younger sister Maria at a dance, no one could do anything to stop their love.

At first, I only guided. Soon, they were studying for parts as if they were preparing for the stage performance of the real West Side Story. Faculty members joined in and began helping students prepare for their try-outs.

Following were members of the drama club: Alphonso Benniefield, Neville Riley, Juel Everett, Phillip Everett, Ivory Shepherd, Rick Lampros, J. Walker, Cindy Allen, Msatio Rodriquez, Miriam Hernandez, Mary Batista, D. Whitley, Tommy Tillis, Steve Johnson, Sherman Harris, Robbie Maxey, Betty McHenry, Charlie Fuse, Esther Boyd, Anthony Boyd, Charlene Nelson, Gwen Boldin, Linda McCray, Phyllis Durham, Melvin Osborne, Jackie Parchment, Kenneth Wright, Harold Howard, Sammie Saxon, Deborah Boyd, William Holloway, Jimmy Williams, Hazel Barber, Rhonda McNair, Lettie Gulley, Keith Babbs, and Debbie Durham.

Sometimes when we became too loud during rehearsals, Principal Scott visited and peeped through the door, or we heard the click of the intercom in our classroom.

Student participation soon caused me to request play rehearsals after school hours in the classroom. After several weeks, however, we were forced to hold play rehearsals after school in the auditorium. Surprisingly, the maintenance men began mowing the grass outside the auditorium at exactly the same time as our rehearsals.

Several weeks into rehearsals, Mrs. Lund, the choral directress, volunteered to teach students the songs from the musical, and Mrs. Gwendolyn Davis, the physical education instructor volunteered to choreograph the dance. Unfortunately, the drama club did not have an extracurricular activity budget to purchase the music or props for a performance.

With no hesitation, the students sponsored a talent show. Each drama club member sold tickets. Remaining true to form, the talent show was advertised as "Pahokee High School – Country, which represented the white students, and Soul represented the black students.

The sale of tickets financed the hiring of one of the most popular white radio announcers in the Glades as the emcee of the talent show. The night of the talent show, because of public safety, the Pahokee Fire Department had to deny entrance to many of the attendees due to building capacity. The students sold more tickets than the building could accommodate. The talent show was overwhelmingly enjoyable and financially successful!

After the talent show, Mrs. Lund purchased the music score, Mrs. Gwendolyn Davis began teaching the dance routine, and the fun began as the music drowned out the sound of the lawn mowers!

As the rehearsals continued, roles began to change among the characters. As the teacher, I had learned not to interfere as long as black and white students were happy and cooperating with each other.

For example, the white student who had been cast in the role as "Riff" was replaced by a black student. The stage crew that once was all white was now completely integrated, and the once interracially mixed cast of "West

Side Story" was now all black. Only one white student remained-Rick Lampbros as Officer Krupke. Alma Henry played Maria. Alphonso Benniefield played Tony. Juel Everett played Detective Schrank, and Robbie Nell Everette played "Anybody."

The students kept working together as if nothing had changed. Not one student missed a rehearsal, and they became amazingly more comfortable with each other.

Friday morning, the day of the performance finally arrived, and the excitement of finally seeing the performance was felt throughout the school! I had proudly relinquished my duty to the music teacher, the choreographer, and the stage crew.

Students

Watching the prompters, Mrs. Lund, Mrs. Gwendolyn Davis and Rick Lampros and his father direct the entire play was easy because everyone knew his or her role, and egos had not yet been practiced nor learned.

Mr. Lampros, Rick's father, built and created two stages: he placed the street scene on one side of the stage canvas and the balcony scene on the opposite side. During the scene changes, the stage crew simply reversed the canvas. The stage crew was magnificent. Even the timing of the all-important gun shot was on cue.

There were two moments at the end of the performance that will remain with me forever. One was the long standing ovation and the other was the show of tears among the student body.

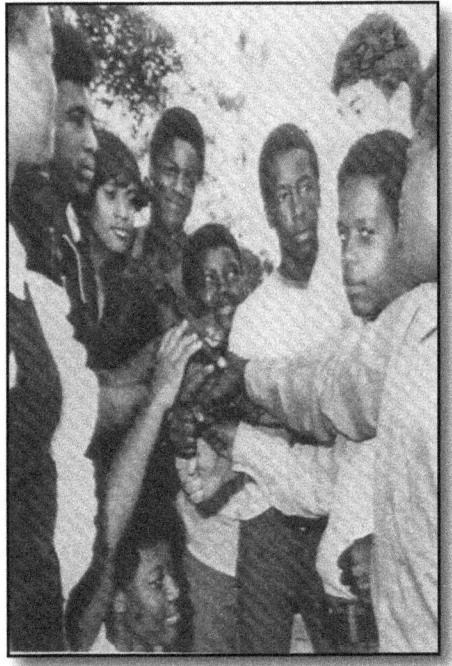

THE JETS
Included in the Photo: D. Harris, C. Williams, A. Henry, K Babbs, K. Wright, R. Lampros, S. Saxin, H. Howard

THE SHARKS
Included in the Photo: D. Banks, A. Bouie, E. Daniels, I. Shepherd, G. Bolden, H. Barber, L. Gulley, C. Bens, R. Maxey, B. McHenry, C. Fuse, L Harris

L to R: Ricky Lampros as Bernardo. Juel Everett as Riff.

The actresses and actors never returned as drama students: they were thespians! It did not take Principal Scott long to request the thespians repeat the performance for the Pahokee community.

I wanted to say no, but it was not my call. So I waited until that Friday and left it up to the actresses and actors of the drama club to respond to the principal's request.

Their response was "No!" They remembered the frequent interruption of the lawn mowers and the perception that Principal Scott initially did not support their efforts.

As the end of the school year approached, my curiosity about the switching of characters was finally answered by Robbie Nell Maxey. The girlfriend of the young man who played Tony did not want her boyfriend kissing the girl who was playing the part of Maria.

At the end of the school year, the drama club enjoyed discussing how to spend their funds from the ticket sale. This now was my time to show these performers just how appreciative and honored I was as their teacher. They had proven that desegregation or Option 2 could be accomplished in the Palm Beach County school system if the adults allowed the students to teach how Option 2 should be introduced.

Now it was my time to reclaim my role as their teacher and give them their just rewards. I received permission from Principal Scott to spend the money from the drama club's budget. Pahokee High School could get credit for having the first "Academy Awards Show" in the city of Pahokee. Each awarded trophy was at least twenty-four inches tall and engraved with the various categories of winners, from "Best Actor" to "Best Floor Sweeper."

The final act was the student body nomination of two teachers as candidates for "Teacher of the Year." The nominees were Mrs. Lund, the music teacher, and Mrs. Greene-Lincoln, the English teacher.

In 1973, the students of Pahokee High School chose Addie L. Greene-Lincoln as Pahokee High School's first black "Teacher of the Year," an honor I will always cherish.

My husband and I relocated from the Glades, to the city of Riviera Beach, but my memories and my heart never left Pahokee High School. My students taught me how important talking and compromising are among people of different races!

After five years of marriage, I divorced and taught one year at Boca Raton High School and four years at John F. Kennedy Junior High School before becoming a full time freshman communications instructor at Palm Beach Community College.

CHAPTER 12

Police and Politics

Most women are depressed after a divorce, but with no money, fortunately, I found comfort making friends, playing tennis, and singing in my church choirs.

Tennis to some people may be an expensive sport, but I did not find it expensive to purchase tennis attire at the Palm Beach Church Mouse, and wearing choir robes on Sundays saved shopping at the malls for new dresses!

In 1977, my finances forced me to seek a part-time freshman communication position at Palm Beach Junior College, which soon became full time under President Dr. Edward Eissey. In 1997, Dr. Dennis P. Gallon, became the first African American president of the college, and under his administration, Palm Beach Junior College became Palm Beach State College.

After teaching several years at Palm Beach Junior College, I sold my home in the city of Riviera Beach and purchased a townhouse in a racially mixed housing development named Tiffany Lakes. Within a few months, I fell in love with the smallness and the quietness of the town and decided this was where I wanted to live.

I joined the town of Mangonia Park's Code Enforcement Board, became active in my homeowner's association, continued playing tennis, and joined Alpha Kappa Alpha Sorority, and several other organizations.

The only thing missing from my life was the car I had dreamed of since the seventh grade.

At that time, there were only two black female Corvette owners in Palm Beach: Rose Darden, the wife of Riviera Beach's first black police chief, William Boone Darden, Sr. and Jackie of Riviera Beach and my soror whose Corvette naturally was green. Addie L. Greene was about to become the third.

My Corvette

Once I drove off the car lot, I became one of the favorite targets of a Mangonia Park Public Safety Officer, Joe Von Dembowski. Officer Dembowski not only changed my life, he changed my future. He ticketed me for not having auto insurance, no inspection stickers, or a driver's license.

During one of my traffic stops, there was no convincing this public safety officer that my last name had been misspelled on my driver's license. The "e" from Greene was missing on my license, but the "e" was printed on my insurance card. The officer gave me a ticket for driving without auto insurance.

Several weeks later, he ticketed me because my Corvette did not have an inspection sticker and my inspection sticker wasn't up to date: two tickets! Deciding I needed help, I met and explained my situation to Earl Mixon, the first and only black man elected to the town council of Mangonia Park. At the end of our conversation, he said, "You already serve on the Code Enforcement Board. You should run for the town council."

Members of the town council met in a church building the town had purchased in the mid 1960's. It was located at 5301 Australian Avenue, which today is home to Shuler's Memorial Chapel.

I knew nothing about reducing crime, police morale, deteriorating property, or the need for more light industry, and I had never heard of racial profiling.

In 1977, we were a small and quiet town of approximately 1,200 residents. The Town's most conspicuous landmark building was the Jai Alai Fronton. We didn't and still don't have a post office or a library.

Soon three council persons were up for reelection to the town council of Mangonia Park: Councilpersons Earl Mixon, Floyd Hoefs and Kathleen Dunham. I filed to challenge incumbent Floyd Hoefs, and another town resident, Juanita Sumerlot, who was also black, filed to challenge Kathy Dunham.

As soon as our campaigns began, race became one of the issues in the election. But the residents of Mangonia Park were motivated on Election Day. More than half of Mangonia Park's registered voters turned out to vote. The incumbent, Mayor Kathy Dunham defeated her opponent Juanita Sumerlot, and they re-elected Councilman Earl Mixon and a newcomer–Addie L. Greene, who won 55 percent of the vote to defeat the incumbent, Floyd Hoefs. I began my term on the council to receive the $100.00 monthly stipend that came with the position.

Nearly 55 percent of the town's thirteen hundred residents cast ballots that Tuesday. In addition to electing council members, the residents approved a controversial referendum that required council members to represent districts. Some residents said the referendum was a way to guarantee black residents at least three seats on the five-council seat. Voters put two blacks, one of them an incumbent, on the five-person council. Supporters were especially concerned because five Mangonia Park councilmembers lived on the same street.

Although elections in Mangonia Park were usually low key affairs, this election simmered as the town clerk sought to track down the identity of a group that plastered signs around the one square mile town urging voters to support the referendum.

The group was illegal because it had not registered as an endorsing group. Candidate Juanita Sumerlot complained on Election Day that the signs she shared with me had been taken down. The town clerk said signs along Australian Avenue and Forty-Fifth Street had been removed by Mayor Dunham and Assistant Clerk Jean Rowland who were familiar with ordinance violations. "It's just a misunderstanding about signs," said the clerk.

MANGONIA PARK TOWN COUNCIL
L to R: Addie Greene, Earl Mixon, Kathalene Dunnam, Gerald Henin, James Carr

The years I served with Councilpersons Mixon, Dunnam, Henin and Carr, motivated me to learn more about the position and the potential to bring about change.

In 1986, I served as the first black female vice mayor of the town. As vice mayor, I was the head of Mangonia Park's public safety department. The department consisted of sixteen certified police officers and two certified fire officers. These individuals were now under my administrative jurisdiction.

In 1986, during my term as mayor, the town council voted to replace the police chief with Officer Joe von Dembowski. After he became chief, he requested a meeting with me and confessed he was the officer who gave me the ticket violations, but he still gave no other explanations, and I required none!

Town engineer John Bills and his staff assist Councilwoman Greene, Mayor Dunham and Councilman Mixon at the ground breaking of their $1.2 million dollar municipal office complex at 1755 East Tiffany Drive, Mangonia Park.

This complex now houses the town's administration and staff, the Town Council meeting chamber and the Palm Beach County Sheriff District II Sub-station, where Lieutenant Louie Colon and Lieutenant Rodney Thomas were officers when I was first elected to the town council.

CHAPTER 13

Burial of Mrs. Ella Bell Colbert

In 1989, my sister Debra Dillard and I had the unfortunate task of burying my godmother and best friend, Mrs. Ella Bell Colbert. Soon after the death of her husband, Mr. Edward Colbert, she was diagnosed with cancer.

Deborah Treadwell-Dillard relocated from Huntsville, Alabama to Tiffany Lake and purchased a townhouse in Tiffany Lake, where she became Mrs. Colbert's live-in nurse.

Her minister and most of her friends and visitors from Belle Glade spent their memorable moments with her while she enjoyed her remaining days with Deborah in Tiffany Lakes. We never gave up trying to get her to cut down on her dips of Red Bull Snuff. After eating her favorite meal of barbecue ribs, she craved her Red Bull. Deborah and I tried to break her habit, until her doctor said, "Why deprive her of her only enjoyment? It isn't going to kill her."

In June 1991, Mrs. Ella Bell Colbert was buried next to her husband, Mr. Edgar Colbert, in the Port Mayaca Cemetery, which is well known as one of the burial sites for victims of the 1928 storm, the third worst natural disaster in American history.

CHAPTER 14

Redistricting in Palm Beach County

Redistricting is the process by which new congressional and state legislative district boundaries are drawn every ten years. In Florida, our 160 state legislators are elected from political divisions called districts.

As the mayor of Mangonia Park in 1992, I received a telephone call from a gentleman who explained that history was in the making because Palm Beach County was seeking a black person to run for a newly created district in the Florida Legislature due to redistricting.

"You and Dr. Gerald Burke were the first two individuals we thought of," said the caller. "Dr. Burke said he didn't want to run for political office, so we would like to meet with you."

To be considered second or third to Dr. Gerald Burke was complimentary in any situation! He is a legendary, well-known and respected educator throughout Palm Beach County. But I faced a dilemma! How could I serve in the state legislature and remain a college instructor?

After speaking to Dr. Edward Eissey, president of the college, the possibility of being a state legislator became more interesting and exciting. He assured me of my positions at the college and the State Legislature would both be assets to the students and the college.

Unfortunately, there were four black women and one white man also hoping to make history: Yevola Falana, Jolinda Herring, Elizabeth M.

Johnson, Olivia B. Simmons and Will Wagner. All four of the black women and the one white man were very credible candidates.

The population of Mangonia Park was approximately 1,500 people, but the population of District 84 was 156,530. This political challenge was certainly a bigger mountain to climb.

I had never hired a campaign manager, never asked for a campaign donation, never formed a campaign committee, and as a graduate of Florida A&M University, had never visited the capitol buildings.

My campaign committee began on my patio with the following individuals: my sisters, former Mangonia Park councilwoman Mary Gray, Debra Carmichael, Lee Williams, Yvonne Peterman and her family, Willie Thomas, Mangonia Park mayor Gayle English and wife, Judy Schultheis, former Mangonia Park councilwoman Seletha Scott, and Councilmember Earl Mixon. We were off to a good start!

We moved from my patio to our campaign headquarters located on Forty Fifth Street in Mangonia Park. Our campaign family grew to over 150, and nearly all had a key to the doors of the campaign office.

Returning from church one Sunday morning, I drove past the campaign office and saw a white Mercedes Benz parked at the back door. The next day, we discovered that the owner of a local construction company had replaced the missing ceiling tiles in the campaign office. A few days later, living room furniture appeared from a local furniture store!

The campaign headquarters became our home away from home. During one of our campaign meetings, a volunteer went into labor and was rushed to the hospital where she gave birth to our campaign baby, whom we named Karess Williams.

After the primary election, Yevola Falana received 15 percent of the vote, JoLinda Herring received 13 percent, Elizabeth Johnson received 11 percent, Olivia Bailey-Simmons received 18 percent, Will Wagner received 7 percent, and I had received 29 percent. Olivia Bailey-Simmons and I were in a run-off.

You would think that the runoff with my opponent, Olivia Bailey-Simmons would have been easy, but she took advantage of her relationship with Congressman Alcee Hastings, one of the most popular black elected officials in South Florida. Suddenly, he became her distant cousin. That was a smart move. Wish we had thought of it!

But Congressman Hastings was also in a tough run-off election. He was being challenged by Lois Frankel. Olivia assumed that Congressman Hasting's race would be an incentive for people to return to the polls, and she would be the beneficiary.

In the end, we did not need the help of a distant cousin. Our victory came from above and from the voters!

The night of the runoff, the entire family of volunteers presented me with a plaque engraved with the following:

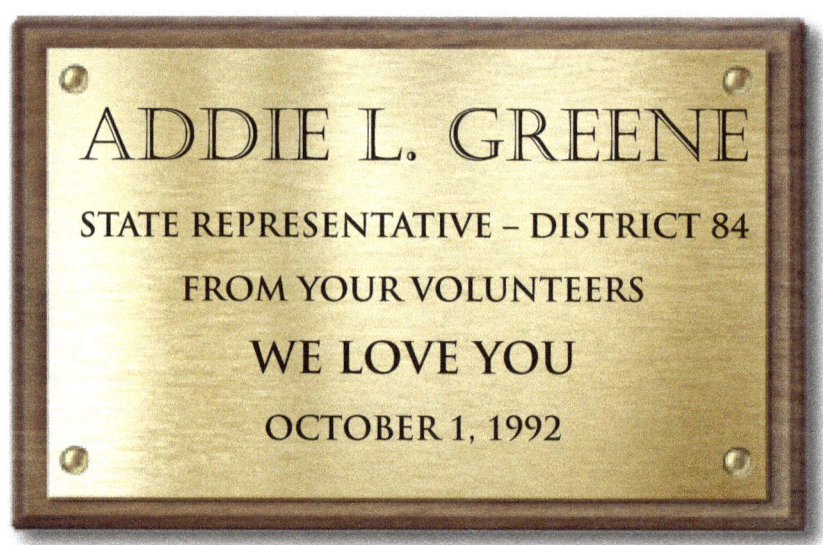

Addie Greene with campaign volunteers and campaign baby

CHAPTER 15

Welcome to the Florida House

Reapportionment dominated the legislative agenda, with representatives more intent on keeping their seats than passing legislation. The final plan was not approved until July 1992, but according to black legislative leaders, the seven month struggle was worth it. Reapportionment worked!

It was my victory in the primaries that helped me to realize the importance of reapportionment. A day after the primary runoffs in 1992, two black congressional candidates joined the November elections. Add the nineteen or twenty blacks who had won seats in the state legislature, and the picture became clearer.

Florida State Representative Willie Logan, a Democrat from the southeast Florida city of Opa Locka said that the reapportionment was just what black candidates had hoped for. Given the chance, black voters were able to elect other blacks to office, no matter how much money the other candidates pumped into their campaigns. It was about time!

If Alcee Hastings and State Representative Corinne Brown were to win their elections on November 3, they will join Representative Carrie Meek as the first blacks to represent Florida in Congress in more than 125 years.

As The Palm Beach Post reported on the elections at that time, reapportionment had the potential to change the fate of black political candidates in Florida.

Democrats Hastings from Miami and Brown of Jacksonville had Republican candidates in their districts in the general election. Willie Logan, the outgoing chairman of the Black Caucus in the State House, said blacks traditionally have been unable to organize and elect candidates because for years their communities were deliberately split among several districts.

The re-apportionment process, which took seven months and spawned countless drafts, was supposed to draw new district lines that would unite minority communities in selected districts to give them a stronger influence over who was elected.

"It was terrible getting here, but the process worked," said Representative Al Lawson, a Democrat from Tallahassee. "We have more access, both here in Florida and in Washington, than we have ever had before. Reapportionment is the chief reason for that."

Representative Lawson predicted that the Florida State Senate would have five black members instead of only two, and the State House of Representatives would see an increase from twelve black members to fourteen or fifteen after the November election. The increase in numbers would include myself, newly elected to the House in a runoff in Palm Beach County and either Matthew Meadows or Billy Brooks in State Senate District 30.

"It is not going to be business as usual in the state legislature," said Lawson, who was at the time the newly elected chairman of the Black Coalition. "We are going to have a pretty strong coalition going. It's going to change the power structure."

For Lillian Gaines, a member of the board of directors of Palm Beach County's chapter of the Urban League, the election of two blacks representing the county in the legislature was is a victory that signaled a new era in Florida politics.

"Maybe this means that everyone will have an equal opportunity at holding office," said Mrs. Gaines. "If redistricting is what it takes to reach that, then it is worth all the wrangling we did."

But with political victories came responsibilities. The pressure was on for those blacks elected in minority districts. Their constituents expected them to deliver.

"Okay, so reapportionment worked," said Rep. Logan. "It is time for them to go up there and deliver."

On November 17, 1992, a young energetic crew from Palm Beach County was to be sworn in along with eight other legislators who would represent Palm Beach County in Tallahassee. We were younger, more energetic, less partisan, and less combative than delegations of the past several years.

"So many of us are new and are anxious to work together," Representative-Elect Suzanne Jacobs, D-Delray Beach, said after her election victory.

"Charged up after months of campaigning, the seven other new legislators and I were scheduled to be sworn in on November 17. Our intentions were to avoid the bickering and occasional lack of unity of previous delegations. You are going to see a more cohesive group," said Rep. elect Mimi Andrews, D. Royal Palm Beach. "We are going to go up there and change government."

Rick Minton, Democrat, Fort Pierce; Tom Warner, Republican, Stuart; Sharon Merchant, Republican, Palm Beach Gardens; Sen. Ron Klein,

Democrat, Boca Raton; Senator Matt Meadows, Democrat, Lauderhill; and Addie L. Greene all Democrats representing parts of West Palm Beach, Riviera Beach and Mangonia Park. We all stood together to be sworn in as members of the Florida Senate and the House of Representatives.

CHAPTER 16

Swearing in Ceremony

According to the rules of the Florida House of Representatives, during the swearing-in ceremony, each member-elect may have only one person sit on the floor next to them. Fortunately, Mom and Dad drove from Birmingham, Alabama to Tallahassee, Florida to witness their daughter being sworn in.

Unfortunately, only one of my parents was allowed to enter the chamber during the ceremony. The decision was left up to them as to which one. I patiently waited and watched the door of the chamber to see which parent I would share this cherished moment with.

Of course, deep within, I knew the decision Dad would make. Finally, I watched the Sergeant–at-Arms escort my mother into the House Chamber. I proudly looked up into the gallery and blew my dad a kiss catching both my parents proudly smiling at each other.

This was my parents' first and last time visiting the state capital. My father died in 2002, and my mother died 2007, both during my term as county commissioner.

Addie's Parents: Mack & Mary Treadwell

CHAPTER 17

Mrs. Janice Stanley

Once dust settled at the capitol and families, friends and relatives returned to their final destinations, I found myself living in a motel and watching some young boys slip through the back door reserved for the paying guests.

The yearly salary of a legislator was $29,697, or $152 a day based on the number of days we were in session. With that income, I knew I could not afford to live in a motel. But even if I could, this situation was a health hazard.

I directed my legislative assistant James Harper, Jr. to search among local African American churches for a widow with no children who would welcome renting to a female member of the Florida Legislature.

Mrs. Janice Stanley, the first black female mail carrier for the city, welcomed me. For eight years at $300 a month, I enjoyed the luxury of the completely furnished upstairs of her home.

CHAPTER 18

District Offices

Each Florida state representative is appointed two District offices: one is located in the state capitol, and the second one is selected by the representative as long as it is within the district to be accessible to the residents.

Accessibility was difficult for the voters in District 84 because of its configuration. It included all or parts of the following South Florida cities: Lake Park, Riviera Beach, Mangonia Park, Loxahatchee, West Palm Beach, a small piece of Palm Beach Gardens and all of Belle Glade, Pahokee, and South Bay. As a result, Pahokee, Belle Glade and South Bay residents lived over one hundred miles round-trip from their district office, and a telephone call was long distance, even though 561 was the area code.

My staff and I decided to do something that had never been done. To serve the three western municipalities-Belle Glade, Pahokee, and South Bay, we asked the Speaker of the House for a third district office.

An emphatic, "No!" was his reply.

But we did not take "no" for an answer to a situation which was obviously an unfair burden on these tax payers! We knew we had to find a way to convince Speaker Bo Johnson.

As a freshman legislator, it quickly became obvious which committees, departments, organizations and groups in the state of Florida carried more weight. One was the Department of Agriculture and Consumer Services. Since the Speaker had made me the vice-chair of this Committee, now was the time to use the position. After conferencing with my staff, we agreed to seek the help of David Goodlett, one of the most respected and popular lobbyists in Tallahassee, who grew up in Belle Glade and was a lobbyist for "Big Sugar," more officially known as the Sugar Cane Growers Cooperative of Florida.

Within a month, the Speaker received a letter from the agricultural community requesting that he send his legislative assistant to visit Belle Glade, South Bay and Pahokee. A week later, Theresa, the Speaker's secretary, arrived at the Palm Beach County Airport on a State of Florida airplane and was escorted to the Glades by PBSO (Palm Beach Sheriff Officers) motorcade, where she was met by an entourage of farmers from the agricultural community.

After her tour of the beautiful farms in Belle Glade, South Bay and Pahokee, she was escorted back to Palm Beach International Airport, and she returned to Tallahassee. Only this time she returned laden with some of the most beautiful vegetables grown in Palm Beach County's incredible fertile soil. Some call this soil "black gold," but it is better known as "the muck."

Along with the vegetables the farmers also forwarded a letter from the Pahokee Chamber of Commerce and Pahokee's mayor, Ramon Horta, addressed to Speaker Bo Johnson, stating that if he approved placing a district office in the Glades, the Pahokee Chamber of Commerce would provide free office space.

District Offices

The historical opening of the office was held several months later in Pahokee overlooking the beautiful Lake Okeechobee, the largest fresh water lake in the state of Florida, the eighth largest natural freshwater lake in the United States, and the second largest natural freshwater lake contained entirely within the contiguous forty eight states.

Diane Walker, another one of my former students and a graduate of Pahokee High School, became and remained the secretary of the office until we were term limited in 2000. After her involvement in state and local government, she decided to seek elected office and was elected a commissioner of Pahokee, where she presently remains.

Ms. Diane Walker - Secretary **Staff Memers James Harper & Juanita Crumity**

CHAPTER 19

Portrait of the Black Caucus

Florida Black Caucus 1993
This is a reprint from the publication *Against the Grain* by Roosevelt Wilson

When I was introduced to the Florida State Black Caucus head of staff, Ecitrym Lamarr and his assistant Miriam Marlow, I realized just why this organization had receiver such recognition and respect from the Speakers of the House, Florida governors, and members of the legislature and the lobbyists.

Attending a meeting of the Florida Black Caucus was like watching a smaller version of the Florida Legislature. People made presentations, and members of the Florida Caucus of Black State Legislators listened and conducted other business at the same time.

The body seemed disorganized and confused as it prepared for the legislative session. But it was a very productive meeting. If the Florida Legislature functioned as efficiently as the Black Caucus did on this particular night, we would never need extended sessions. Representative Al Lawson, president of the Black Caucus, steered his fellow lawmakers through the multiple item agenda expeditiously, with a firm, but gentle hand. His colleagues followed his lead.

Frankly, I was pleasantly surprised by the degree of harmony, humility, sense of common purpose and unity in a room filled with so many egos. The group discussed some major issues, and not once was there an argument or a hostile response. Members had their differences of opinion, of course, but the differences were not great enough to yield even heated debate. Without exception, caucus members talked their differences through to some resolution. Every action they took, and every motion they passed was with unanimous approval. That was a very healthy sign, one that should have been comforting to caucus members' constituents throughout the state. Without a doubt, the 1993 Black Caucus was united, and where there is unity, there is strength!

The full House and Senate, then and now must prepare for some battles against a unified Black Caucus, when it comes to issues affecting minorities. It was obvious that the caucus was prepared to use its collective strength and votes in such battles. We could not underestimate the historical significance of having fourteen black representatives and five black senators in the legislature at that time, and we shouldn't underestimate the Black Caucus members now.

While the fourteen members in the House obviously could not pass or defeat any legislation without help from other non-black legislators, that number became very significant on any controversial vote. So the non-black legislators who needed those fourteen votes at some point down the line had to be wise enough to realize that befriending the Black Caucus made sense then, and it made good political sense now.

Blacks in the Senate carried even more clout. Although they numbered only five senators at that time, it was 12.5 percent of the entire Senate. With the Senate split along party lines, the black senators' votes were capable of carrying more influence than their small numbers implied.

For the first time since Reconstruction, blacks in the Florida Legislature didn't have to ask for handouts from the legislature. They had sufficient numbers to be a force in the political fray. The bottom line is the caucus was no longer a voice in the wilderness, and as long as some of the caucus members didn't develop amnesia and forget who sent them to Tallahassee, the black caucus would be a powerful and effective voice for minorities.

President Barack Obama and Addie L. Greene

CHAPTER 20

The Rosewood Massacre

It was that we pursue common legislative issues and fight for social and racial justice, issues that had lain dormant in the legislature because of race, partisanship and politics. Due to how the Florida Legislature had ignored and handled minority issues over the years, we did not find it difficult to discover two issues that would historically change the future of minorities and the state of Florida: the Rosewood Massacre and One Florida.

Trouble began when white men from several nearby towns lynched a black Rosewood resident because of unsupported accusations that a white woman in the nearby town of Sumner had been beaten and possibly raped by a black drifter. When the town's black citizens rallied together to defend themselves against further attacks, a mob of several hundred whites combed the countryside hunting for black people. They burned almost every structure in Rosewood.

Survivors from the town hid for several days in nearby swamps until they were evacuated by train car to larger towns. Although state and local authorities were aware of the violence, no arrests were made for what happened in Rosewood. The town was ultimately abandoned by its black residents and none ever moved back.

Although the rioting was widely reported around the United States at that time, few official records documented the event. Survivors, their descendants, and the perpetrators remained silent about Rosewood for decades. Sixty years after the rioting, the story of Rosewood was revived in the mainstream media when several journalists uncovered it in the early 1980s. Soon thereafter, survivors and their descendants organized to sue the state of Florida for having failed to protect Rosewood's black community. But before the compensation, the Florida Legislature commissioned a report on the massacre. As a result of the finding, Florida became the first state to compensate survivors and their descendants for damages incurred because of racial violence.

In 1993, the Speaker of the Florida House of Representatives commissioned a group to research and to provide a report by which the equitable claim bill could be evaluated. On December 22, 1993, historians from Florida State University, Florida A & M University, and the University of Florida delivered a hundred page report on the Rosewood massacre.

In 1994 Black and Hispanic legislators in Florida took on the Compensation Bill to provide $150,000 in compensation to the handful of survivors of Rosewood victims for their property and refused to support Governor Lawton Chiles health care plan until he put pressure on the House Democrats to vote for the bill. The legislature passed the bill, and Governor Chiles signed the Rosewood Compensation Bill.

CHAPTER 21

One Florida

Governor Jeb Bush's decision to dismantle affirmative action in state college admissions, government contracts, and hiring led to a confrontation with the states' black community. Governor Bush described Florida's affirmative action policies as "stupid" and "destructive." As the governor, he decided to end affirmative action in Florida by executive order 99–281. He replaced it with an initiative called "One Florida."

Under Governor Bush's new plan, students in the top 20 percent of each public high school class would be guaranteed admission to one of the State's public universities. On the contracting side, Bush's order wiped out set-asides and price preferences for minority-owned-businesses. Instead, Bush sought to increase diversity procurement by streamlining the certification process for minority vendors and encouraging purchasing officers to reach out to minority businesses.

Lance de-Haven-Smith, a political scientist at Florida State, stated, "Governor Bush caused Blacks to feel their interests were being subordinated to the political interest of the Bush family. It was a very highhanded way to make a very controversial decision." Black legislators complained bitterly of being left out of the process of a policy that would have a significant impact on their community. "He never talked to me. He never talked to any African-American that I knew about," said

Representative Les Miller, who served as the Democratic minority leader at the time. "It was a slap in the face!"

Senator Daryl Jones, chairman of the state Black Caucus, used One Florida as a rallying cry to register black voters ahead of the 2000 elections.

To fully implement One Florida, Bush needed the State University System Board of Regents to approve his ban on racial consideration in state college admissions. In a twist not lost on Bush's critics, the regents' vote was scheduled for Friday, January 21, the week of Dr. Martin Luther King Jr. Day.

A few days prior to the vote, in a last-ditch effort to convince Bush to scrap his plan, the Black Caucus met with Lieutenant Governor Frank Brogan at the state capital to make their case. During the meeting, Bush briefly popped in and told the lawmakers that if they were waiting for him to rescind his executive order, "They might as well get some blankets," according to the Orlando Sentinel. Senator Kendrick Meek and State Representative Tony Hill responded by staging a sit-in on the spot.

The protest was a public relations disaster for Bush, with newspapers likening it to the civil rights demonstrations of the 1960's. As Senator Meek and Representative Hill camped out in the executive office suite into the evening, a couple of hundred protesters gathered outside the capitol building, singing We Shall Overcome. Governor Bush ordered his aides to "throw their asses out." The remark was caught on video in time for the nightly news.

The protest lasted into the next afternoon, ending only after Bush promised to delay the border regions vote by a month. During that time, a panel of legislators held three public hearings on One Florida. The regents ultimately voted to implement Bush's One Florida plan but the protests continued.

After that, Bush "definitely tried" to mend relations with the African American community, notes de Haven-Smith. A few months after the massive One Florida March in June 2000, Bush signed the creation of a law school at the historically black Florida A & M University.

CHAPTER 22

Why & How a Bill Becomes Law Remembering Sister Alberta Burden

As a member of Mount Olive Missionary Baptist Church under the leadership of Reverend A. C. Evans for twenty-two years, Sister Alberta Burden was known by the members of Mt. Olive as "Birdie."

In memory of Mrs. Alberta Burden who made history in 1994, her name was inscribed in law libraries in the state of Florida within the Victim Witness Protection Protocol of "Mrs. Alberta Burden."

Remembered as a "soft-spoken, religious grandmother," she became a martyr whose murder motivated the state of Florida to set up a witness protection program to protect women, men, and children from harm.

Ms. Burden was a witness in the murder of one of her close relatives. The alleged murderer was a member of a well-known gang known as the Parson Gang. This gang was one of the most notorious gangs in existence in Palm Beach County.

The state attorney for Palm Beach County wanted to place Mrs. Burden in a witness protection program. The program would pay for her protection until the murder trial. However, at that time there was no such program in existence in Palm Beach County. The only place the state attorney could go to get such a program set up and funded would be the Florida Legislature.

As the representative for the City of Riviera Beach, I was honored to make sure the Witness Protection Program law carried Mrs. Alberta's name.

The Parson Boys were a drug-dealing gang that made a lot of money selling drugs when crack cocaine was king. The Parson gang reportedly brought in approximately $200,000 a week. It seems as if everyone knew of the gang, but no one could touch them, including law enforcement.

Beginning around 1985, they operated out of a city owned park in West Palm Beach. They eventually expanded the family business into Tallahassee, where a $20,000 kilo of Columbian cocaine powder would sell as crack on the streets for more than $50,000.

One official called the breaking of the Parsons Gang, the one case that helped bring down West Palm Beach's most feared and prolific crack cocaine ring.

Alberta was shot to death in her car, just as she was preparing to testify that the murderer of her goddaughter was the goddaughter's husband and the leader of the Parson gang. He had gunned her down because of a domestic dispute three months earlier.

After five years, the Palm Beach County prosecutor closed out Alberta Burdens murder case, lamenting the lack of evidence and handed out plea deals that meant a combined sixty years in prison for three gang members.

"Though the State originally sought the death penalty against the Parson Gang trio, all were lackeys in what was once a $200,000.00 a week distribution operation," said prosecutor Chuck Burton. He said he had little recourse but to close out the case before going to trial. He had no physical evidence he claimed, and no eyewitnesses to the September 1994 murder of then sixty year old, Mrs. Alberta Burden.

"The only evidence that defendants James Grimsley, 38, Kenneth Wilmot Young, 27, and Kelby Ramon Franklin, 26, carried out the hit order on Burden in order to silence her testimony was the testimony of fellow gang members," Burton said. All those witnesses were facing long federal prison terms on drug conspiracy charges, and they wanted reductions in their sentences in return for their cooperation.

Prosecutor Burton was not ready to pay that price, he said. Instead, the members received plea deals all approved by Circuit Judge Marvin Mounts Jr. Kenneth Young was sentenced to spend forty years in prison for firing the five shots that killed Mrs. Burden as she pulled into the parking lot of a West Palm Beach mental health center to report to work.

James Grimsley, who police say drove Mr. Young to the scene of the murder, would serve a fifteen year sentence. Mr. Young, known as Choo-Choo to his friends, and Mr. Grimsley pleaded guilty to the lesser charge of second degree murder.

Kelby Franklin, who allegedly shelled out $6,000 in Parson's proceeds to pay Young and Grimsley pled guilty to accessory after the fact. He was sentenced to five years, though that would have no effect on the life sentence he received that would send him to federal prison on drug conspiracy charges.

"I'm not particularly thrilled with the sentence compared to the leniency shown to the others," said Young's attorney, Glen Mitchell. But because his client was facing the possibility of being executed for the crime, Attorney Mitchell advised Young to accept the plea.

It was Burden's murder and the murder of her goddaughter that brought heated law enforcement scrutiny to the Parson Gang's sophisticated drug operations. The spotlight ultimately led to the convictions of eighty individuals, including family members and associates in federal court in 1996 on drug distribution charges.

Those convictions effectively shut down the drug ring, sending the key operators to prison for life. But the fear and intimidation the gang invoked in some of their West Palm Beach neighbors may be lingering today.

An example of the intimidation was on display during the trial when the state Attorney's office asked two neighbors to testify in Mrs. Burden's murder trial. Both individuals refused, saying they feared for their lives. "Their reputation is still there, even if they are not," Palm Beach County state attorney Barry Krischer said at the time.

After Mrs. Burden's death, State Attorney Krischer helped influence the state legislature to approve a witness protection program, similar to the federal model that provides government money to put witnesses in safe houses. Though such programs were not available at the time, police say that Ms. Burden took moderate precautions in protecting her safety, knowing she could be a target for retribution from Thomas Parson Jr.

Just three months earlier, according to the police, she watched Parson shoot her goddaughter in the front yard of their Riviera Beach home as she was packing the car and preparing to leave him.

Neighbors and relatives warned Mrs. Burden about the dangers of testifying against Parson, the reputed gang leader of what prosecutors called a gang of "urban terrorists."

Mrs. Burden did take precautions. At the mental health center where she worked, she began parking closer to the building and using the side entrance. Her co-workers also kept an eye on her as she walked to and from her car. But the parking lot was empty at 7:30 a.m. on the day of her murder in September 1994. According to the police, Young and Grimsley drove up to Mrs. Burden's car as she pulled into her usual spot.

"Young fired off five shots," Prosecutor Burton would later reveal. Mrs. Burden was found slouched over the front seat of her car, clutching her Bible. Her pocketbook lay untouched beside her.

Dumas Parson, one of the leaders of the gang, was immediately suspected. However, he was never charged with ordering the hit. He did not even face trial for the murder of Thomas' wife. But while in the County jail on other charges, Thomas Parson became too sick to stand trial for anything and he eventually died of AIDS-related complications.

"I've been doing this for 20 years, and I've never had a witness murdered to shut her up," said State Attorney Krischer. "So this was a big deal." *Sun Sentinel February 12, 1999- By Nicole Sterghos Brochu, Staff Writer*

Defining the Witness Protection Program

The witness protection program is just what its name implies. It is a program for individuals who have agreed to serve as witnesses for the government. In some situations, their testimony puts their lives in jeopardy and sometimes, the lives of their family.

In witness protection programs, the protected individuals are moved to a place where they are least likely to be found. It may not be the most glamorous place, but they are safe. If this is a permanent move, the people are given jobs and small allowances until they can sustain themselves. They are also be given new social security numbers, new names and birth certificates. This is for extreme cases.

Some individuals who enter the witness protection program are never allowed to speak with family or friends. It is as if they died and all things that were tied to their lives are now changed and destroyed.

CHAPTER 23

House Page and Messenger Program

Students between twelve and eighteen years old are chosen by their senator or representative from their district to serve in the Page and Messenger Program in the Florida legislature.

The students work in the capitol and surrounding buildings with their senators and representatives Monday through Friday from 8:00 a.m. to 5:00 p.m. and are paid a stipend of $100 a week.

As time allows, Pages and Messengers participate in optional tours and educational activities, which may include a week mock session, observing a live committee meeting, touring the governor's mansion, the Florida Supreme Court, the Museum of Florida, and the historic capitol.

Any student involved in the program that bullies another student, either physically of verbally, will be asked to leave the program and may have their stipend or service hours revoked.

Rep. Greene with a legislative staff member and Messengers
This photo originally appeared in the Palm Beach Post newspaper

CHAPTER 24

The Palm Beach County Commission

Maude Ford Lee

Due to term limits, eight years were winding down for certain members of the Legislature. In 1998, some members were already seeking positions after term limits. The only office I could seek was the Palm Beach county commission. However, that position was presently held by the commissions' only black member, Maude Ford Lee, who had been in office for a decade and had a strong core of black Democratic supporters. She was also very respected and popular in the black community and all of Palm Beach County. Her supporters were so committed to her, that they were known as The Lee Machine. It would take a campaign like no other to topple this entrenched incumbent.

As an incumbent, she had a tremendous advantage in raising campaign money. Most of all, she had an aura of invincibility. She had represented the district since it was created in 1990, and no challenger had come close to beating her. I had never run against such a strong candidate.

What helped convince me to challenge her was her decision to seek reelection in 2003. If she won, her term would expire in November 2004. This mattered because she had signed up for a Florida early retirement program that would pay her a lump sum of up to $10,514, plus a monthly pension of $3,302.00 when she left office. But this was predicated on her leaving office by November 30, 2003. She would forfeit the entire lump sum and get a much lower pension if she stayed in office one day longer.

Mrs. Lee sought an opinion from the attorney general's office as to whether she could remain a commissioner and get her pension if she chose not to accept her Commissioner salary for the final year of her term. She hoped that the section of state law pertaining to the early retirement program would allow her to stay in the elected position and essentially serve as a volunteer.

If Commissioner Lee had received a favorable opinion from the attorney general, I would not have signed up to challenge her. My decision not to run would have eliminated a headache for the county Democratic Party Chairman who called Mrs. Lee's pension dilemma "a serious problem" for Democrats. If she left office in 2003, the republican governor had the authority to appoint the person to complete her term.

With no Republican eyeing the post, the primary winner would move directly onto the board of commissioners, representing an approximately forty mile stretch of the county from Riviera Beach to Delray Beach, an area primarily east of Interstate 95, which was heavily democratic.

My stunning 173-vote victory over Commissioner Lee was the result of an innovative strategy that targeted Republican voters, who were primarily white as well as white Democrats. We also made a strong effort to snare black Democratic voters in Riviera Beach and West Palm Beach. Lastly, Mrs. Lee and her team ran a very expensive campaign one that I think was plagued by overconfidence.

"Lee ran a good, strong campaign and she had nothing to be ashamed of," said Mikel Jones, an advisor to U.S. Representative Alcee Hasting and a long time Lee supporter. "But Greene had a different strategy. That's what won," he said.

My name was as well-known to voters in Riviera Beach and the black neighborhoods in West Palm Beach as Commissioner Lee's because they were part of my district during my eight years in the state legislature.

Because of a new state law that allowed Republicans to vote in Democratic primaries when there was no Republican candidate, our campaign garnered thousands of new voters. My campaign consultant always felt that if we targeted Mrs. Lee's base of supporters and brought in new voters we could build a winning ticket.

However, it was not easy to harness those voting blocks. Mrs. Lee and I both considered the black Democratic voters in Riviera Beach and West Palm Beach our political base. However, my approach was simple.

My campaign spent day after day in the neighborhoods, knocking on doors and reminding residents of my record in the legislature. Election results showed our grass-roots appeal worked. In Riviera Beach, we received 51 percent to Commissioner Lee's 49 percent. I also targeted the white Democrats and Republicans on the wealthy island of Palm Beach and in West Palm Beach using a flurry of direct-mail ads in the final weeks of the campaign. Commissioner Lee had largely ignored those folks. The results were decisive: predominantly white precincts supported my campaign 64 percent to Lee's 36 percent.

I only raised $36,336, far less than the $83,399 raised by Commissioner Lee. But my campaign used our funds for direct-mail instead of a campaign office. We only had two campaign consultants on payroll, at a cost of only $4,500. So we had to use our money effectively.

Mrs. Lee spent nearly $12,000 for twenty one workers listed as "professional" or "consultant services" on her campaign finance reports. We held onto our money until the last minute and it seemed to work.

The talk around town was that I made some high profile attempts to woo the wealthy, white Palm Beachers during the primary. We did target those voters, but the critics did not know that it was the concentration on other largely ignored smaller communities like Lantana and others that helped us achieve our slender victory.

For example, in the town of Lantana there was a special town council election with three important ballot questions that coincided with my election. Since Lantana's residents were coming out to vote in their local election, we made an effort to win their vote for me. It worked! I won in Palm Beach as well. Nevertheless, it was a close race. I won by a 1.6 percent margin.

Legislative assistants Shirley Meeks, Sharon Battles, Commissioner Greene and Aminta Culmer

The Palm Beach County Commission

L to R: Senior Assistant Rosetta Rolle, Secretary Juanita Crumity, Legislative Assistant Gladys Whigham, Commissioner Greene, Legislative Assistant Michelle Andrewin, Senior Assistant Danzell Holmes. Not shown: Barbara Hardnett

To establish a better relationship with the community leaders, voters, and elected officials in the South County District, our first priority was to re-open the South County District 7 Commission office. Each county commissioner had two district offices, and the second office in South County made me more accessible to my constituents in that area.

The following photos show some constituents and elected and civic leaders who joined us in the opening of our South County office.

FROM THE COAL MINES TO THE BOARD ROOM

Commissioner Addie Greene and
Boynton Mayor Gerald Broening

Commissioner Addie Greene and
Lantana Mayor David Stewart

Commissioner Addie Greene and
Delray Beach Mayor David Schmidt

Commissioner Addie Greene and
Hypoluxo Mayor Kenneth Schultz

The Palm Beach County Commission

South County supporters welcome Commissioner Addie Greene

Dr. Andre Fladell, Comm. Alberta McCarthy, Comm. Greene, Mayor Tom Lynch

CHAPTER 25

The Beginning of the Palm Beach County Caucus of the Black Elected Officials

Palm Beach County Caucus Black Elected Officials

As a former vice mayor, mayor, and college professor was admirable, becoming the secretary of the Florida Conference of the Black State Legislators was easily one of my most honorable and exciting accomplishments. I quickly became efficient in using the linguistics of the legislature, including terms such as "placed on the calendar," "amendments," "House committee rules," "suspend the rules," "pass a bill," and more.

But when the bills went to the "floor" for debate, is was then that I realized how excellent debaters most members of the Black Caucus were and how inefficient I was because I was never taught the rules of debating.

This was just one of many challenges I faced and overcame that encouraged me to return to Palm Beach County and organize the Palm Beach County's twenty seven black elected officials into a powerful and effective voice for minorities of Palm Beach County.

As the County Commissioner for District Seven, I was proud the beautiful Morikami Museum was located in District Seven. With the help of the manager of the museum, each black elected official was invited to attend a private luncheon at the beautiful museum and Japanese garden located in Delray Beach. The luncheon was historical because it was the first time ALL black elected officials as a group had visited the museum.

Thanks to the Palm Beach Post and the Sun Sentinel newspaper reporters, Palm Beach County was finally introduced to its black elected officials.

Palm Beach County Caucus of Black Elected Officials, Inc.
2000-2002

Chair: County Commissioner Addie L. Greene
Vice Chair: Mayor Steve Wilson. Belle Glade
Secretary: Commissioner Retha Lowe. Lake Worth
Assistant Secretary: Vice Mayor Lorraine Griffin. Mangonia Park
Treasurer: Councilperson Elizabeth Wade. Riviera Beach
Assistant Treasurer: Commissioner Carl McKoy. Boynton Beach
Historian: Commissioner Alberta McCarthy. Delray Beach
Parliamentarian: Commissioner Isaac Robinson. West Palm Beach
Accountant: Mrs. Zenora Ward, CPA. Ward and Company
Consultant: Mrs. Mami H. Kisner

The Beginning of the Palm Beach County Caucus of the Black Elected Officials

In preparation for our first black tie gala scholarship fundraiser, the board of directors suggested we meet with Mr. Donald Trump and request the Mar-a-Lago resort facilities. But the date, time and place where we were to meet made the front page of the Palm Beach Post before we met.

The headlines the next day read, *Bitterness over Greene's Win Refuses to Fade.* More than eight months after Greene ousted Maude Ford Lee from her Palm Beach County Commission seat, bitterness lingers in some corners of District 7. Worshipers at several black churches eight days ago returned to their vehicles to find flyers accusing Greene of creating a disgraceful image for black elected officials by wining, dining and socializing with Donald Trump.

Accompanying the flyer was a copy of a to-do list I had typed to remind me of my scheduled activities. On the list was the date and time we were to meet at Trump's Mar-a-Lago club in the fall to host the Black Caucus scholarship gala celebration.

Commissioner Addie Greene, Donald Trump, Former Supervisor of Elections Teresa LePore and Black Caucus member Michelle Andrewin

Our tour of Mar-a-Largo was two-fold. As a sitting County Commissioner, Donald Trump needed my vote for his new golf course, and the Palm Beach County Caucus of Black Elected Officials wanted to premiere its first black-tie gala in a formal ballroom setting at Mar-a-Largo.

During our tour of Mar-a-Largo, Trump welcomed us to his ballroom. But when we entered the dining area, we saw a tent instead, because the ballroom was being renovated. I thanked Mr. Trump and told him his tent was not the type of venue we desired.

Several days later, we received a call from famed local attorney, Robert Montgomery offering his assistance. Because of his influence and generosity, our first black tie-gala was a sold-out affair at the luxurious Palm Beach Four Seasons. In addition, Mr. Montgomery and his beautiful wife, Mary Montgomery opened their home for our unforgettable reception.

Boxing Promoter Don King attends Black Caucus Gala

The Beginning of the Palm Beach County Caucus of the Black Elected Officials

Black Caucus members present scholarship check to deserving student

2000-2014
Palm Beach County Black Elected Officials, Inc.

Mayor William Albury
Supervisor of Elections Arthur Anderson
Mildred Anderson
Michelle Andrewin
Mayor Clarence Anthony
Commissioner Keith Babbs
Deputy County Adm. Verdenia Baler
Dr. Emma Banks
Sharon Battle
Commissioner Esther Berry
Commissioner Allie Biggs
Sylvia Blue
Clifford Bridges (Deceased)
Mayor Michael Brown
Roseann Brown
Commissioner Johnny Burroughs
Michael Carn
Beatrice Coleman
Councilperson Peggy Cook
Vice Mayor Henry Crawford
David Dangerfield
Councilperson Judy Davis
Councilperson Terrance Davis
Councilperson Norma Duncomb

2000-2014
Palm Beach County Black Elected Officials, Inc. *(cont'd)*

Port Commissioner Dr. Jean Enright
Articia Futch
Evelyn Garcia
Councilperson Lawrence Gordon
Commissioner Angelita Gray
Commissioner Addie L. Greene
Commissioner Linda Hamilton
Theo Harris
Congressman Alcee Hastings
Commissioner Woodrow Hay
Vice Mayor Felecia Hill
Commissioner Gwen Holly
Councilperson Lynn Hubbard
Councilperson Ann Isles
Commissioner Alson Jacquet
City Commissioner Keith James
Councilperson Sarita Johnson
Commissioner Mary Kendall
Don Kerbos
Commissioner Joe Kyles
Jacquet LaFontant
Jean Joseph Lexima
Commissioner Retha Lowe
Councilperson Shelby Lowe

2000-2014
Palm Beach County Black Elected Officials, Inc. *(cont'd)*

Mayor Thomas Masters
Commissioner Carl McCoy
Commissioner Mack McCray
Commissioner Taranza McKevin
Sandra Mapp
Shirley Meek
Nadja Neptune
Commissioner Fred Pinto
Senator Bobby Powell
Rita Powell
Port Commissioner Wayne Richards
Claude Rigaud
Miquel Rios
School board member Dr. Debra Robinson
Elizabeth Robinson
City Commissioner Isaac Robinson Jr.
Gloria Shuttlesworth
Councilperson Earl Smith
Tony Smith
Lourdes Stacey
Caneste Succee
Commissioner Janet Taylor
Commissioner Priscilla Taylor
Councilperson Cedric Thomas

2000-2014
Palm Beach County Black Elected Officials, Inc. *(cont'd)*

Jacqueline Torcchom
Mayor Colin Walkes
Earlene Weston
Gladys Whigham

CHAPTER 26

Palm Beach County Caucus of Black Elected Officials 2013 Newly Elected Officers

President: Riviera Beach Councilperson Terrance Davis
First Vice President: Port Commissioner Dr. Jean Enright
Second Vice President: Riviera Beach Councilperson Cedric Thomas
Secretary: Mangonia Park Councilperson Addie L. Greene
Assistant Secretary: Clewiston Commissioner Janet Taylor
Treasurer: Pahokee Vice Mayor Felisia Hill

Historian: Florida State Representative Bobby Powell, Jr.
Parliamentarian: Haverhill Councilman Lawrence Gordon
Sergeant-at-Arms: Belle Glade Commissioner Johnny Burroughs
Chaplain: Pahokee Commissioner Allie Biggs
At-Large Member: Dr. Mildred Anderson (Deceased)
Executive Director: Elizabeth P. Robinson
CPA: Mrs. Zenora Ward and company
Consultants: Mrs. Mami Kisner and Mrs. Sandra Bridges

CHAPTER 27

Black Caucus in Disarray: Scholarship Cash in Limbo

The following article is a reprint from the Palm Beach Post, December 2017:

Addie Greene founded the Palm Beach County Caucus of Black Elected Officials in 2003 with the best intentions.

A county commissioner at the time, and a former state representative, she recalled recently that when she first entered the state capitol, she knew nothing of the legislative process. She never had a class in debating or any other skills needed to succeed as a lawmaker. "I felt so incompetent."

Fourteen years later, the organization she formed to promote black leadership, award scholarships and help others overcome their unfamiliarity with the system is in disarray, idled after being placed in the hands of Riviera Beach Councilman Terence Davis. The organization that once had more than three dozen members has none, its money sits in a Bank of America account that former members can't access, and high performing high school seniors who were promised scholarships aren't getting them.

Davis, 41, a city councilman since 2003, faces a recall election over the firing of a popular city manager without explanation. He did not return calls requesting comment for this story.

Belle Glade City Commissioner Johnny Burroughs, to whom Davis told others he turned over the account, also did not return calls. Greene and other former members say they've been unable to get either Davis or Burroughs to account for the money the group raised for students.

An investigation by West Palm Beach Police found no probable cause to believe the money – as much as $30,000 by Greene's estimate – was stolen. Assistant Chief Tameca West said she subpoenaed the bank, found the account intact and satisfied herself that checks had been written for scholarships and nothing improper.

She advised Greene, who had gone from the State Attorney's Office and Palm Beach County Sheriff's Office to the West Palm Beach police with allegations of potential embezzlement to consult an attorney about how to retrieve the money from the dissolved nonprofit's account. Greene plans to consult with other former caucus members before hiring a lawyer.

"Terence Davis…he's done with it," said West, who did not recall the exact mount left in the account. "He wants nothing else to do with the organization. But the money's sitting there in the bank. If he's not cooperating with Greene, it could be because he's tired of being called a thief," she said.

But Greene isn't the only one to lack confidence in Davis. Jean Enright, vice chairwoman of the Port of Palm Beach, was vice president of the caucus. She said she worked hard for years to raise scholarship money through Palm Beach galas and other means and wanted to know it was available for its intended purpose. Burroughs told her he has all the money but would not provide records, she said.

We had an accountant who did everything for years. When Terence became president, he said, "We don't need it.' He was given pertinent books and records…I asked him to turn over the records to Addie. He told me he was not going to do it because she was no longer in office."

From its inception, only the accountant, Zenora Ward, was authorized to write checks on the organization's account. Ward did not return messages requesting comment. It's not clear who, if anyone was authorized to disburse the money after her departure. That's the problem because scholarship winners were told they would get $1,000 a year for four years and some were still owed money at the time the state dissolved the organization in 2015. The state pulled the plug after the caucus' registered agent resigned and Davis didn't replace her.

Because caucus records were in Davis' hands and he won't make them available, neither Greene, Enright nor other former leaders of the organization know how many scholarship winner were left high and dry. One winner's parent confirmed to the Palm Beach Post that the caucus still owes the student money but the parent didn't want details disclosed.

County Commissioner Mack Bernard, caucus president immediately before Davis, said the organization played such an important role in training elected officials as a well as awarding scholarships that he had been talking with Greene about reviving its mission, if not the organization itself.

The question, he said, is whether to form an entirely new group, because without records and without knowing what liabilities the old organization incurred, it would be too risky for new people to join.

"We need to move forward," Bernard said. "There are major issues the caucus can take on to improve the lives of the residents of Palm Beach County."

Written by Tony Doris the Palm Beach Post Staff Writer. 12/4/2017

CHAPTER 28

Deputies Call for Greene to Resign

The following article is a reprint from the Palm Beach Post, August 2005:

Palm Beach county commissioner Addie Greene found herself in a familiar spotlight last week when a grand jury cleared a white police officer in the shooting death of a black teenager. As the lone black person on the seven member commission, Greene was expected by many white and blacks alike to speak out on any matter of interest to the county's nearly two hundred thousand black residents. It's a role Addie Greene has both resisted and embraced in nearly five years on the commission. While saying she dislikes being pigeonholed as the county's black Commissioner, Addie Greene said she feels obligated to address issues her white colleagues ignore.

"When there is a black issue like this, people look to me for leadership and that's what I'm supposed to do. I don't like it, but that's the system," said Greene, who represents a district with a plurality of black voters.

She was the only elected official on hand last Wednesday when the South County branch of the NAACP held a news conference to decry the grand jury's clearing of Delray Beach officer Darren Cogoni in the death of sixteen-year old Jerrod Miller. *(George Bennett - The Palm Beach Post. 2005)*

In the political career of most elected officials, especially minorities, unforeseen circumstances occur. However, tragedy involving the death of a young black male brings on a unique and tremendous responsibility. In this chapter, the death of a cheerful and helpful sixteen year old young man named Jerod Miller with a promising career took the focus of my political career to a different and futuristic level.

A few months past his 16th birthday, Gerard Miller longed for manhood. Throughout the beginning of 2005, the Delray Beach teenager had been searching for part-time work in his hometown, but landing a first job is more difficult if you are a black teenager.

Tall and lanky, with short cropped hair, Jerrod had a tendency to freeze up during confrontations, but he was popular with the girls. He had kept on the straight and narrow, with a passion for computers and activities at church, where he earned a reputation for helping elderly parishioners.

On the cool Saturday evening of February 26, 2005, Gerard probably felt more man than boy behind the steering wheel of his uncle's 1988 Cadillac. Although he failed his written driver's license test a few months earlier, Jerrod managed to finagle the Cadillac from his uncle from time to time, despite objections from the boy's grandmother, with whom he lived. As far as she knew, Jerrod was Miami bound that night for a church – league basketball game.

Jerrod cruised the neighborhood instead. Several times, he picked up teens who asked for a lift to the dance at a local high school. The school was hosting a dance in the gym for 12 to 16 year olds. Just before 9 p.m., Jerrod motored into the west gate and pulled the Caddy up beside the gym; several teens hopped out. Only about 20 kids had actually paid their five dollars to get into the dance at the time, while others mingled outside waiting for friends to arrive.

Darren Cogoni, a baby faced, 23-year-old rookie cop with the Delray Beach Police Department, stood near the gym entrance and took special note of the car. He'd seen a similar vehicle gunning its engine and squealing its tires about 15 minutes earlier on the street running past the school. Cogoni and his partner, Kenneth Brotz, both of who are white, walked toward the car. Both men were working for the school on off-duty detail, but they were armed and dressed in full uniform.

Many have imagined what Gerard was thinking as Cogoni stepped up to the driver's side door and asked the young man for his driver's license. Much of what is known about the case comes from a statement given by Cogoni hours later.

Cogoni described Jerrod as *"fidgety"* and *"nervous."* Brotz, who stood near the front driver's side fender, recalled the boy being *"jittery"* and repeatedly stammering, *"I'm just, ahh..."* Jerrod bowed his head. Cogoni took one step backwards as he continued to ask Jerrod for identification and rested his right hand on the butt of his holstered .40 caliber Glock. Undoubtedly feeling panic, Jerrod suddenly gunned the car, and Brotz stepped back out of the way of the side mirror. Several teenagers scrambled up the gym's steps as the Cadillac barely missed grazing them.

Cogni scrambled after the car, with Brotz not far behind. Jerrod turned left widely and pulled between two buildings that formed a breezeway. Although this passage wasn't intended for vehicles, Jerrod raced on, the car scraping loudly as it bounced from side to side against the walls. Cogoni charged after it, pulling his hand gun out of the holster. Stopping about 12 feet behind the car, he said he saw a large group of people at the end of the breezeway.

"I was close enough to see the head rest of the drivers' seat through the back window, and I was able to see a silhouette of a head, of the driver," Cogni said later. "I couldn't see any passengers in the vehicle."

He took aim and fired two shots. One of the bullets plowed into the back of Jerrod's head and lodged just behind his left eye. Gerard likely died instantly, and the car continued forward until it slammed into a cement retaining wall.

The Palm Beach Post – 2005

REDEMPTIVE LIFE COMMUNITY MEETING

As I took the podium and looked at the audience, the year was 1965, and I was at Stillman College attending a planning meeting at the First African American Baptist Church on Stillman Boulevard in Tuscaloosa, Alabama.

On this particular day, the church was attacked and canisters of tear gas were thrown through the church windows. Women were beaten with Billy clubs while trying to escape by jumping out of the Church windows. There were members of the clergy, black community activists, black elected officials, members of the NAACP, the Urban League, and even some members of law enforcement. The message was the same: We shall overcome racism. We sang uplifting songs, we prayed, and there were angry messages about the injustices and the unjust killings of not just black teenagers, but Black people.

Now, it is 2005, and I am the county Commissioner standing at the podium in another Baptist church in Palm Beach County because of the unjust killing of another black teenager. Then I remembered a television commercial Florida law enforcement officials made several years ago. Its message to women and men was not to stop when asked to pull over until they are in a well-lit place.

With tears running down my cheeks, I took the microphone and said, "When our black men are pulled over by a police officer, they should drive to the brightest place they can find with the biggest crowd of people. If they don't, they will be murdered!"

The following Tuesday, August 23, 2005, members of the Police Benevolent Association (PBA) wrote in the Palm Beach Post that they had a problem with an elected official encouraging black youth who were approached by officers to run and find the biggest crowd of people.

Law enforcement took the public's attention off the shooting of a black teenager by a sheriff deputy and placed it on me telling black boys to run when stopped by law enforcement. However, once law enforcement was away from the public's eye and confronting me, their attention was on my use of the word "murdered" instead of "killed."

The fact that these words were not my words or that I did not tell young black men to run was not important. What mattered and what was successful was the unjust death of Jerrod Miller!

That following Monday, I denied saying black men should run. I stated that news stations began the broadcast with my comments with the run which gave the false impression I wanted youth to disobey police officers.

Months passed as state attorney Barry Krischer delayed his decision as to whether or not criminal charges would be filed against Cogoni. Then, in July 2005, Krischer unexpectedly sent the case to a grand jury, which convened in private, and a month later released its decision not to indict Officer Cogoni.

The initial fury over the shooting of Jerrod Miller metastasized into general cynicism among some of Delray Beach's black citizens. The thirty-one member Black Community Task Force, which formed during a period of unity after Jerrod's death is now largely dormant, but the reasons it came into existence in the first place live on.

In June 2005, the task force sent a memo outlining the race related issues it believed that the city must face. To be Black in Delray, the memo began, is to live in a constant state of rage.

Local black leaders and the NAACP joined together to turn the anger into action. They committed to act on the issues voiced by the community. Those issues included the need for a citizen police review board, change of the use of force policy, recruitment of black officers, increased funding for city parks, and economic development.

Delray Beach Mayor Perlman agreed to meet with the task force, but then the mayor formed his own committee, which he said was necessary because the NAACP and the task force could not agree on what they wanted.

The city immediately hired an outside consultant to review the police department's use of force policy, which was expected to be completed later that year. The advisory committee also recommended forming a citizen's committee to make recommendations to the police chief, but it would possess no investigatory or review powers. Perlman viewed this as the will of the black community, as expressed through the advisory committee.

Jayne King, a member of the black task force had a different take. "People perceive this was his way of setting up a kind of shield, to have no direct confrontation," said King in referring to the Mayor's actions.

The NAACP's Martin described the mayor's advisory committee as comprised of former elected officials, people that worked directly for the city in some capacity, or received city grants. It was what I call conflicts of interest. The mayor's committee did not include people in the community who really felt affected by racism.

Regardless of the perceptions of what the city was doing or not doing, the deepest furrow of cynicism over Jerrod's death was by the state attorney's office. Under intense public pressure, state attorney Barry Krischer announced in March that he'd requested a public inquest with a straight – forward objective: determine if probable cause existed to charge Cogoni in the death of Jerrod Miller. After one false start, in which a judge recused himself for possible conflict of interest, the inquest job fell to Deborah Moses Stephens, a black judge who had been a public defender in the past. After presiding over a three-day, packed-to-the-walls hearing in April, Judge Stephens determined that the shooting death wasn't a justifiable use of deadly force by a law enforcement officer and that probable cause existed to charge Cogoni with manslaughter.

What became clear to everyone listening to the testimony was the fact that none of the over thirty witnesses had seen anyone standing in front of Jerrod's car as he drove down the breezeway. Not even Cogoni's partner could say for certain there was someone in harm's way.

Months after the inquest, Jerrod's grandmother was still perplexed over Cogoni's actions. "I have yet to understand how anyone could shoot someone in the back of the head that's driving a car and say they feared for the lives of kids that were in the way of the car. If you disable a driver of a car, the car is now out of control. So now the kids' lives would be truly in danger," she said.

Judge Stephens' decision wasn't binding for Krischer, who as a former defense attorney had represented police officers in cases involving excessive use of force. So as weeks turned into months after the inquest, a mood of skepticism spread. In late July, Krischer announced that he'd be sending the case to a grand jury, the same secretive process that the inquest was intended to replace, critics said. Krischer's primary stated reason was that Judge Stephens had based her decision "in part on hearsay and other inadmissible testimony."

The grand jury chose not to indict Cogoni. However, the city of Delray Beach fired him immediately, an action that many thought was overdue, but that only kindled more ill will.

"I think it was a fulfillment of the cynical expectations of the black community," King said. "There is no justice served. It's just another of the same old tactics for the white man to be in power. The people in the justice system were going to protect their own."

Even Mayor Perlman was nonplussed. "I think there was a lack of leadership from the state attorney's office on this issue," he said. "Why do one inquest? I just don't understand why it played out the way it did."

For many blacks in Delray, the answer was apparent. "There was no way that Barry Krischer, while he was state attorney, would make a police officer go to jail for killing a black man," one black activist commented. "He never had in the past; he never would in the future. He took the political way out with the grand jury."

All during this investigation you would have thought the attention would have remained on the shooting of a young black man and the outcome of the investigation. That was not the case. Every day on the six o'clock news, in the Palm Beach Post, or even when black and white residents talked over the picket fences, the topic was always the same thing: County Commissioner Addie Greene told young black men to run.

Finally, my staff scheduled a news conference on the twelfth floor of the government center for me to attempt to again clarify my remarks. We invited elected officials, community activists, members of my church, and others to attend. A group of fifty to seventy five people quietly walked with me down the hall toward the conference room. When we opened the doors, every chair in the room was occupied by white police officers, with the exception of one lone-black officer sitting obviously in the center of the crowd. Each officer wore a T-shirt that read, Addie Must Resign!

Suddenly, their stone-faced stares of pure anger filled the room, especially from the face of one particular young officer who sat in the first seat on the first row. His face personified pure pent-up hate that needed no interpretation. Being familiar with their looks, I knew my words "to run," were not the cause of their anger; it went deeper than that.

Unshaken, I stepped to the microphone and attempted to read my apology, but their childish boos and looks of intimidation made it almost impossible! Within minutes, the event deteriorated into a shouting match

Greene defiant as officers call for her to quit

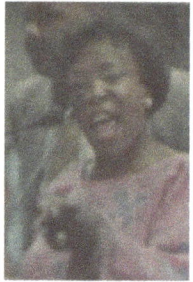

Commissioner Addie Greene responds to comments from a group of mostly white officers at the end of her news conference Monday morning.

Officers that called for Greene to quit

between the white men in the white T-shirts and some of my present supporters.

In attendance was Former Riviera Beach mayor Michael Brown who eventually was forced to escort me and my staff back to our office, but not before I told a news reporter my opinion of the men we saw in that room: "The only things they left at home were their sheets!"

At that moment, I vowed not to apologize. The event ended peacefully, with the deputies booing like high school children. Again, I knew it was not just about the words "to run" it was about the word "murder!"

CHAPTER 29

Palm Beach County Days

Fortunately, several weeks later, my staff and I were relieved when we traveled to the capital for the annual celebration of Palm Beach County Day. For two days, county municipalities and representatives promoted the county's legislative issues and priorities that were most important to the future of Palm Beach County.

It was also an opportunity to reunite with staff, visit the Florida A&M University campus, and to enjoy two fun-filled days socializing and lobbying members of the House and the Senate for their vote on projects and funds for Palm Beach County.

As I checked into the Doubletree Hotel, an African American deputy, who was also a member of the Palm Beach County Caucus of Black Elected Officials, approached me.

"Commissioner Greene, could you meet me in the conference room of the hotel at 6:00 p.m. this evening for a few minutes?" he asked.

I replied, "Sure," without any hesitation.

Promptly at 6:00 p.m., I approached the conference doors. Once I pulled them open, it was as if I had re-visited the twelfth floor of the Palm Beach County's conference room. Facing me again were some of the same evil white faces, but without the white T-shirts, except there were more of them!

This time there were men wearing law enforcement wearing uniforms, and suits with white shirts and ties, and some officers were dressed casually. Reporters were absent, but the atmosphere was the same: hostile!

Unbelievably, John Kanzanjian, the union president of the Police Benevolent Association, began where he left off from my press conference in Palm Beach County. Only this time, his topic was my use of the word "murder."

He began to explain why I should not have used it and why. He stated "murder" meant "to kill unlawfully."

In other words, he was implying that I had determined Officer Cogoni to be guilty of unlawfully shooting sixteen year old Jerrod Miller.

By now, these officers had taught me how to count to ten, how to control my anger, and how to not respond to them. I left the conference room with a smile, but not before I informed them that as an English professor, my vocabulary was not the same as the law enforcement or an attorney. So my definition of "murder" and "kill" were the same. This time I exited the room alone.

John Kazanjian had publicly stated, "I would love for Commissioner Greene to resign, but she's not, and we can't make her."

My friends and family urged me to ask for county protection as a result of the union's hostility, but I felt this was no longer about Commissioner Addie L. Greene. This had become about law enforcement hoping to take the public's attention away from the handling of the grand jury by state attorney Barry Krischer. He was determined that Cogoni would not be charged or convicted in the shooting of Jerrod Miller.

Palm Beach County Days

Even though the 2005 shooting death of Jerrod Miller became the most incendiary of any incidents during my political career, the grand jury did not indict white Delray Beach Police Officer Darren Cogoni in the February shooting death of Jerrod Miller. **Written by Mike Clary- The Sun-Sentinel**

It wasn't long after this event that I began receiving racist hate mail under the moniker "WOC," which meant "White Officer's Club." Within several months, my name was returned to the headlines in the Palm Beach Post. "Greene satisfied with plan to ask FBI to investigate racist mailings." I wanted the county to hire a private investigator to figure out who was sending me racist hate mail under the moniker "WOC."

The sheriff's office and the state attorney spent three consecutive years investigating the hate mail. Even after I spoke to county attorney Denise Neiman whose office planned to ask the Federal Bureau of Investigation to investigate the messages, the hate mail increased every day.

Then I began receiving messages which included images of Senator Barack Obama with a noose around his neck. The messages also suggested that I should be hanged.

One day, the sheriff's detectives identified a sixty six year-old Lake Worth black man named Robert Haynes Jr. who had sent me at least two racist postcards. But prosecutors declined to file charges against him though the sheriff's office sought to have him arrested on a misdemeanor count of stalking. The Sheriff office even wasted time sending the mail to the US Secret Service, according to the sheriff's spokeswoman, Terry Barbera. Despite the hateful messages, prosecutors said Mr. Hayne's writing contained no threats and didn't break the law. **Written by Jennifer Sorentrue- The Palm Beach Post.**

The Palm Beach County Police Benevolent Association endorsed my opponent, former Riviera Beach councilwoman Elizabeth Wade, in the November election.

The PBA's endorsement of Elizabeth Wade actually helped me win votes during my next campaign.

CHAPTER 30

Scripps Research Institute

Commissioner Addie Greene sits with former Florida governor Jeb Bush and then- governor Charlie Crist at the dedication of the Scripps Research Institute Florida campus in 2007.
PHOTO REPRINTED FROM THE PALM BEACH POST

March 10, 2007 was a breezy Saturday. Against a backdrop of construction and partially erected buildings, I joined former Governor Jeb Bush that morning as he passed his vision of the Scripps bioscience hub in Palm Beach County to his successor, Governor Charlie Crist. In a thirty-minute ceremony, we joined local leaders and scientists to formally dedicate

The Scripps Research Institute's Florida campus, officially putting to rest years of delays, setbacks and legal challenges that had sidelined this biotech giant.

"Without Jeb Bush's vision, without his leadership, without his tenacity and without his integrity, we would not be sitting here today," Governor Crist told the crowd. "What this place to me represents is a place of hope."

First, let me tell you how this story began and why the city of Jupiter was the chosen location for Scripps bioscience Research giant.

Although there were seven county commissioners, former Governor Jeb Bush and State Senator Jeff Atwater, along with other members of the Florida legislature discussed the location of Scripps with only six of the seven county commissioners. The lone black commissioner, Addie L. Greene, was not privy to what Scripps was or its future location in Palm Beach County.

I only became aware of Scripps the morning it appeared on the commission agenda. As I entered the chamber, Deputy County Administrator Verdenia Baker pulled me aside and began to excitedly tell me about something called "Scripps."

"Commissioner Greene, this could become Palm Beach County's Disney World!" she exclaimed!

During the meeting, I listened to County Administrator Bob Wiseman, Deputy County Administrator Verdenia Baker, scientists, staff, lobbyists, representatives, and others discuss a division of the Scripps Research Institute.

I soon learned that Scripps was a state-of-the-art nonprofit biomedical research facility located in La Jolla, California. The institute utilized the latest cutting edge technology with a focus on basic biomedical research and development of new drugs. The governor was attempting to convince Scripps to relocate to Palm Beach County and also convince the taxpayers to help convince them with *310 million!*

After months of meetings and discussions, Commissioner Jeff Koons and his family took the lead and arranged to jet all seven county commissioners and George Bennett of the Palm Beach Post to La Jolla, California, to tour the Scripps facilities. As the airplane flew through the clouds, George Bennett suddenly asked each of us who would run the county if something happened to the jet. I am happy to write that I do not remember if there was a response to his question.

The vote on where to build the Scripps Research Institute turned out to be a great, unintended political consequence. I became the swing vote as to Scripps Research Institute's location. When I realized I held this newly possessed power, I wanted to use it wisely for the benefit of black businesses and all minorities in Palm Beach County.

As the debate continued as to where to locate Scripps, I revisited the lack of care and support minorities had received during many county building projects as well as major public and private developments in District 7 and throughout Palm Beach County.

For example, the new state attorney's office, the new county court house, and the convention center were all built with very little minority business participation. I saw this project as an opportunity for minorities to finally control at least some avenue of economic development.

The meetings became extremely intense! Eventually, I was forced to stop accepting telephone calls if the topic was Scripps. For my vote, I was offered recreational centers named after me, jobs, dinners, and more. But the most frightening was when I discovered that someone had found a way to place a tracker on my county-issued vehicle! The person finally stopped following me after he or she discovered I frequented restaurants alone and held most of my meetings in the county office.

Careful not to violate a law, I created my personal think tank which included some of the most highly respected and trustworthy community advocates and elected officials in the county.

Clarence Anthony is a graduate of Florida Atlantic University with a Bachelor's Degree in social science and a Master's Degree in urban planning. At that time, he was the senior vice president of Post Buckley Schuh & Jernigan, Inc., as an engineering consultant.

Mami Kisner received her Bachelor's Degree from Marshall University and assisted businesses and nonprofit organizations in fundraising and marketing. Her background is in training, teaching community relations, marketing and sales. She is a board trustee of Florida Atlantic University and the advisor and consultant to the Palm Beach County Caucus of Black Elected Officials, Inc.

The late Roy Mouton was the owner and CEO of American Modular, Inc., which was a Loxahatchee base storage unit supplier. He was a member of the Palm Beach County Business Development Board.

Paul Nunnally holds a MBA from Duke University and was the president of Savant Ventures, a management consulting firm.

Mangonia Park Mayor William Albury held a Master's Degree from Florida A&M University. Mayor Albury is an agent with the State of Florida Healthcare Administration.

Dr. Deborah Robinson is a member of the Palm Beach County School Board. She has a Bachelor's Degree in biology and a Medical Degree from Howard University. She is a practicing medical doctor in Palm Beach County.

Greene's 'think tank' of advisers

Clarence Anthony
Personal: 45; bachelor's degree in social science and master's degree in urban planning, Florida Atlantic University.
Professional: Senior vice president, Post Buckley Schuh & Jemigan Inc., an engineering consulting firm.
Political: South Bay city commissioner since 1984, mayor since 1985; president, Florida League of Cities, 1995; president, National League of Cities, 1999.
Civic organizations: 2005 John S. and James L. Knight Foundation's Palm Beach Community Advisory Committee; Economic Council of Palm Beach County Inc.

Mami Kisner
Personal: 53; Royal Palm Beach resident; the wife of Rev. Gerald Kisner of Tabernacle Missionary Baptist Church in West Palm Beach.
Professional: Consultant assisting businesses and nonprofit organizations in fund-raising and marketing; background in training, teaching, community relations, marketing and sales.
Political: Assistant campaign manager for West Palm Beach mayoral candidate Joel Daves, 1999; appointed by County Commissionaer Addie Greene to the Solid Waste Authority Citizens Advisory Committee.
Civic organizations: Palm Beach Atlantic University board of trustees; former Hope House board president; National Association of Women Business Owners Glass Ceiling Award, 1988.

Roy Mouton
Personal: 60; Loxahatchee resident; born in Lafayette, La.
Professional: CEO, American Modular Inc., a Loxahatchee-based storage unit supplier; president, Kailan Intyernational Consultants Inc.
Civic organizations: Greene's appointee to the county's Business Development Board.

Paul Nunnally
Personal: 36; suburban West Palm Beach resident: master's degree, Duke University.
Professional: President, Savant Ventures, a management consulting firm.
Civic organizations: A founding director, Black Chamber of Commerce of Palm Beach County; Palm Beach Atlantic University Students in Free Enterprise business advisory board; governor, Leadership Palm Beach County.

William Albury
Personal: 45; raised in Boynton Beach; degree in sociology, Florida A&M University in Tallahassee.
Professional: State Agency for Health Care Administration, state Medicaid program.
Political: Mayor, Mangonia Park. In 2003, former Town Manager Michelle Adrewin sued the town, claiming she was fired illegally. The town won.
Civic organizations: Former publicity director for the Homeless No More Center Inc. in Boynton Beach.

Debra Robinson
Personal: 49; raised in Flint Mich., West palm Beach resident; bachelor's degree in biology, Michigan State University; doctor of medicine, Howard University.
Professional: Primary care physician, VA Medical Center in Riviera Beach.
Political: Member, Palm Beach County School Board since 2000.
Civic organizations: Former president, Coalition for Black Student Achievement.

The members of my think tank met quietly for at least a month to craft strategies and goals for the future of minority business enterprises in Palm Beach County. To prepare themselves, they worked together and toured the potential Scripps' site. They reviewed the proposals, sat in on briefing sessions with county staff, offered opinions and asked question after question.

During their tours, these six leaders presented a proposal to the Florida Research Park of a minority business component that would give opportunities to black businesses. This would include economic incentives in training and incubator businesses.

According to Mayor Albury, the residents at that time were at a disadvantage because they didn't have a spokesperson, someone who would make sure that the people benefitted. "We are here to try to set up a framework to ensure that such development benefits everyone," said think tank member Mayor Albury. "Commissioner Greene is a free and independent thinker. She is going to vote how she sees fit."

Paul Nunnally added, "From an historical standpoint, most black folks have not participated in the economic growth in Palm Beach County. What we have done is created a matrix of what we felt were the most important factors to consider. This is not just focusing on black people enumerating goals. Commissioner Greene is clearly interested in how this impacts everyone, the entire county, those in her district, and those in the black community. There are numerous factors we are using to evaluate the sites: attainable housing, transportation, environmental considerations, ability to help the biotechnology and business clusters. We are challenging the

Scripps suitors to do some creative thinking of their own. They know their resources."

South Bay Mayor Clarence Anthony, a well-connected mayor and veteran of county governmental affairs, said, "We have got to find a way to have Scripps, as well as the business community as a whole, reinvest in Palm Beach County's most struggling communities. PBS-&-J [Clarence's company] has no dealings with any of the potential sites being considered for Scripps. My role in advising Commissioner Greene is strictly as a longtime friend. I don't have a preferred site. But if I had one, I would probably change every day based upon the information."

Roy Mouton chimed in. "Commissioner Greene is a very courageous woman. I don't know how she does it, but she has worked very diligently for the minority base. She's done a hell of a job."

Dr. Debra Robinson wanted to ensure that Scripps' impact on local education went beyond helping a handful of right-out-of-high school students. She said her focus was on biotech across the continuum, not just in high school. "I don't think I'm supposed to say much more," said Dr. Robinson. "I was told when we embarked upon this process it would not be publicized."

Sunshine Law Violation

It was the secrecy surrounding my decision-making process that caused some grumbling. The secrecy gave the public appearance of a shakedown. To this allegation, I said, "When black elected officials are in violation, it's a shakedown, but when white elected officials are involved, it's a negotiation."

However, Barbara Petersen, president of the Tallahassee-based First Amendment Foundation, said the meeting of my think tank violated Florida's government in the Sunshine Law because I had delegated part of my decision-making process to the think tank. Barbara Petersen went on to say that if the think tank had been meeting in secret, some of those meetings were subject to the Sunshine Law.

Palm Beach County attorney Denise Neiman said the Palm Beach County state attorney's office would review the matter, but at first blush, she did not believe the group was subject to the Sunshine Law or that any violations had occurred. There was so much factual information that had to be obtained before a conclusion could be drawn.

That Friday, I told Attorney Denise Neiman I was keeping my thoughts on how I would vote to myself. Even the think tank members didn't know how I was going to vote.

Commissioner Mary McCarty stated, "Let me tell you right now. The way this thing is playing out, Commissioner Addie Greene is holding the future in her hands."

The discussion of the location of Scripps was held before a large viewing audience and at a critical point in the high-profile, $510 million biotech venture. All eyes were on me, the commission's lone Black member, who held the deciding vote in February on where the project would be built.

My critics argued that I sold my vote to the highest bidder, and alleged I ultimately took a bribe in exchange for voting for North County's proposal. An ethics complaint filed recently by Russell Yeager of Delray Beach claimed that I misused my position to solicit a gift in exchange for my vote.

Unshaken by the criticism, I remained steadfast in my belief that I acted in the best interest of my constituents when picking the Florida Atlantic University Briger tract site based on a developer's $5 million pledge.

Ethics experts said I did nothing wrong as long as I did not receive something in exchange for my vote that benefitted me personally. My actions weren't any different from those of my fellow commissioners, who had negotiated with developers on behalf of the residents they represented. Whenever someone came before us, we made sure they did what we wanted them to do, or we didn't vote for it.

With the help of the six black leaders who served as my advisers, I used my unique position to benefit minorities. Commissioner Marcus made the motion for the county to negotiate a deal to move Scripps's headquarters to northern Palm Beach County, and I seconded the motion. The north county site won the Scripps prize by a 4-3 vote.

I still don't understand why my vote cast six weeks ago attracted so much attention. I remained upbeat and tried to focus on the positive. It also became an educational issue with my constituents. My sister and the minister of my church didn't even know what Scripps was until Valentine's Day. People in the streets needed to know the $510 million of their taxes was from them.

By Deana Poole/Palm Beach Post Staff Writer

CHAPTER 31

Blacks, Whites Need Right Leaders

This is a reprint from the Palm Beach Post written by Lisa Cramer

It's been called the end of an era, the death knell to a monolithic movement that has been in its last throes for too long. There is a clarion call for re-evaluating whether there remains a common purpose in the struggle for civil rights.

The deaths of icons Constance Baker Motley, Vivian Malone Jones, C. Dolores Tucker and Rosa Parks started the contemplation. "We are at a crossroads," said Civil Rights leader and Georgia Congressman John Lewis. "We can either go forward or stand still."

The funeral last week of Coretta Scott King confirmed the end of the "black leaders." Even Tavis Smiley, who next weekend will host his seventh annual televised State of the Black Union conference from Houston, is using the term "black influencers."

At least in recent decades, particularly as new generations of blacks received unprecedented opportunities to earn college and graduate degrees and higher salaries, buy homes, open businesses and get elected to public office, the media-driven concept of a "black leader," a single spokesperson purportedly for all black people has been inexact and often troublesome. Comedian Wanda Sykes put it this way on TV Land's *That's What I'm*

Talking About Black History Month series: "Don't get me wrong, I love Rev. Al (Sharpton)...We need Rev. Al, but ... if something happens, and then the media says, "We're going to go to the black leader,' and it's the Reverend Al up there, I'm just like,' Oh, please, don't say nothing crazy."

Countless blacks understand what Ms. Sykes means, having to unfairly carry the burden that we represent everyone who shares our skin color and, even more burdensome, that we are represented by anyone who shares our skin color. But anyone who doubts the diversity of the nation's 39.2 million blacks and the still crucial value of African– American thought-leaders, opinion-makers, voices or activism–choose your semantics should tune into C-SPAN Feb. 25 as the *State of the Union* is discussed.

In this area, proof of the continuing need for leaders who are mindful of the disparities between minorities and whites came Tuesday.

Vice Chairwoman Addie Greene, the lone African American among the seven Palm Beach county commissioners had the privilege and challenge of being the swing vote to decide where the Scripps Research Institute will build its Florida home. As the lone commissioner whose district spans the coast of the county, including residents in ten of the County's thirty seven cities, Addie Greene had the responsibility to try and make Scripps mean something to everyone in her district. It should have been a common goal of all commissioners.

Commissioner Greene's decision before Tuesday's vote to enlist the advice of some smart, accomplished friends has been criticized for its secrecy. But what successful person does not have and need mentors, trusted truth tellers, and a sort of personal "think tank," as she described her group? Her effort sounds more objective and potentially less threatening than the typical elected official's frequent, undisclosed private phone calls, lunches, dinners, parties, and meetings with lobbyists, realtors, newspaper editors, developers, and other decision makers.

Commissioner Greene's unflinching demand for a financial commitment to help improve economic development among the county's minorities has been criticized as nefarious. But her valid attempt to spread the return on the public's $510 million investment in Scripps simply solidified what everyone from the governor on down had professed that Scripps's presence would benefit all of Florida.

Handled correctly, the $8 million pledged to minority scholars, businesses, and other initiatives to help even a playing field that historically has been tremendously imbalanced will be good not just for the black community but for all of Palm Beach County.

Commissioner Addie Greene has been criticized for having a black agenda. "In fact, black people want what all Americans want: fair and equal opportunity to realize dreams," said the commissioner.

Blacks who are in positions of leadership will be accused of championing a so-called separate agenda until every leader shares the responsibility of also representing blacks.

Elisa Cramer, Palm Beach Post

CHAPTER 32

Paragon Florida, Inc.

Serving • Supporting • Sustaining Small Business

BUSINESS READINESS

President and CEO— Pamela Stewart

The Board of Directors
Chair—Keith James
Deputy County Administrator Verdenia Baker
Frank Hayden David Harris
Paul Nunnally
John Oxendine
Hansel Tookes
Zenora Ward

WHO WE ARE

Founded in 2006, Paragon Florida, Inc. is a certified Community Development Financial Institution (CDFI) and relending intermediary of the U.S. Small Business Administration dedicated to providing comprehensive loan programs, training and management and technical assistance to businesses in Palm Beach County, FL.

Paragon fills a vital niche in the local financial market by offering small business loans to businesses who are unable to obtain funding through traditional lenders. By affording access to capital and business services, Paragon increases the capacity of businesses and residents to improve their quality of life.

MISSION DRIVEN
A LITTLE MORE ABOUT WHAT WE DO

Small Business Loans assist traditionally underserved businesses obtain access to capital. Paragon provides loans between $10,000 and $200,000 to qualified businesses seeking start-up, growth or expansion capital.

Training is key to success! Paragon offers many educational opportunities and resources for small businesses and entrepreneurs. Educational opportunities include classes, workshops, conferences and seminars.

The **EPICenter** provides a full-service **Co-Working Space** where like-minded entrepreneurs and business support agencies connect, collaborate and flourish!
- Affordable Class A Office Space for Businesses & Partners
- Workbench with Secure High Speed Internet
- Networking Events and Business to Business Discount Program

Counseling and Technical Assistance is routinely provided to businesses applying for loans.
- One-On-One Counseling (Free)
- Mentoring and Management and Technical Assistance

IMPACT

|  | | | | | | |

$1,325,000 capital deployed | 158 jobs created | 2,150 entrepreneurs trained | 535 businesses counseled | 32 new businesses created

SunTrust, Bank United | Comerica Bank | PNC | Knight Foundation | CDFI Fund | U.S. Small Business Administration | Community Foundation of Palm Beach and Martin County | City of Rivera Beach CRA | Lake Worth CRA | West Palm Beach

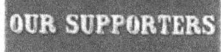

Paragon Florida, Inc. | 400 Hibiscus Street | Suite 200 | West Palm Beach, FL | 33401 | 561-282-1888 | www.paragonfl.org

CHAPTER 33

No One Has to Die from Breast Cancer

This chapter is dedicated to
Survivor - **Mattie Myrick-Robinson**
April 18, 1944-Feb. 22, 1986

Mattie Myrick, Addie Greene and Daisy Brown-Lanier

In 1976, Alex Haley wrote *Roots - the Saga of an American Family*. His grandmother told him stories about their family that went back to her grandparents and their grandparents down through the generations all the way to the man she called "the African."

During the seventies, this movie's emphasis on African American heritage caused family reunions in African American families to flourish nationally. Even today, seldom in the black family will you pick up a family Bible and not find a family tree.

Unknowingly, family reunions are future life savers for black families. Unfortunately and regrettably, black families no longer emphasize their family heritage or the family tree.

Before 2007, I knew very little about my family's medical history. When I was five years old, my father abandoned my mother, my three brothers: Tom, who was six, Nathaniel who was four and Harry was three years old and me at the age of five.

Whenever we asked our mother about her mother or father, she always responded that they were dead and Grandma and Grandpa Boglin raised her and her two brothers. She said one brother died of tuberculosis, and one died by drowning. Soon, we stopped asking.

In our schools from the forties to the seventies, vaccinations were mandated against hooping coughs, mumps, measles, smallpox, and rubella. There were few to no prevalent medical conditions or childhood diseases I was aware of in my family. In other words, I grew up assuming I was a member of a very healthy family. So my answer to the standard medical history questions, "Is there a family history of any of the following: high blood pressure, glaucoma, arthritis, diabetes, sickle cell, keloids, epilepsy, cancer, heart attack, Alzheimer's, or tuberculosis?" was always a proud, "No."

However, in 2007, that all changed when I was serving as county commissioner. At the advice of the orthopedic surgeon, I visited my primary care physician, Dr. Anita Wilborn, to schedule a complete physical examination in order to build up my strength for knee surgery.

I completed the physical examination and returned to my office. A week later, I received a telephone call from the doctor's office to return for a second opinion: I had stage one cancer in my right breast!

As I drove around the hospital, I needed someone to talk to. No one in my family had ever been diagnosed with cancer, and my mother was in the final stage of Alzheimer's!

Before I realized it, I had returned to the office of Dr. Anita Wilborn, who presently was my primary care physician. I signed in and patiently waited and prayed! When my name was called, I walked into her office, and I knew she was aware of my results. Without mentioning my diagnosis, she asked, "Do you want to talk to Dr. Henderson?"

I took a soft breath and thought to myself, "Finally, a woman I can talk to!"

As I entered the office, I was surprised to see that Dr. Henderson was Dr. Raymond Henderson! He immediately noticed my surprise he was a male and not a female physician. But within minutes, I knew the names of his beautiful daughters and his wife as he pointed to each of their framed photos. He began to share with me his daughter's bout with breast cancer.

I left his office with a smile in my heart. I knew he would be the surgeon to remove the cancerous growth from my breast. I felt as if I had spent an hour talking to my mother! As I turned to exit his office, he said, "Commissioner Greene, no one has to die from breast cancer!"

The news of my cancer reached my brothers and sisters and also the family of my lost father. Ida Mae Garner, my cousin by way of my biological father, told me about her brother who died from prostate cancer.

The year after my diagnosis, my sister-in-law Bobby Nell Greene convinced my brother Tom to take his long over-due physical examination. Thank God for her perseverance. The doctors discovered Tom had first stage prostate cancer.

Because of early detection, he is still surviving eight years after his diagnosis. Unfortunately, in 2012, he developed Alzheimer's. With his wife's excellent home care and the community programs of the Alabama Alzheimer's Foundation, he is enjoying life between his home and the excellent Alzheimer's day-care facility.

Finally, it is extremely important to know your family's medical history. It gives you valuable information about your close relatives. A family medical history can identify people with a higher-than-usual chance of having common disorders such as heart disease, high blood pressure, stroke, certain cancers, and diabetes.

It provides information about the risk of specific health concerns; however, knowing your family's medical history does not mean that an individual will definitely develop a condition in that history. A person with no family history of a disorder may still be at risk of developing that disorder.

Knowing one's family medical history allows family members to take steps to reduce their risk. For people at an increased risk of certain cancers, healthcare professionals may recommend more frequent screening such as mammography or colonoscopy starting at an earlier age. They may also provide regular checkups or testing for people with a medical condition that runs in the family. The easiest way to get information about family medical history is to talk to relatives about their health. A resource for much of this information is the US National Library of Medicine.

Finally, on August 29, 2016, I had my left knee replacement performed by Dr. Gregory Martin, one of Palm Beach County's best orthopedic surgeons on staff at John F. Kennedy Hospital in Atlantis.

Dr. Elizabeth McKeen, and nurse practitioner Deidra Brown-Brinson, ARNP of the Florida Cancer Specialists Institute in Palm Beach Gardens, have been important members of my breast cancer support system.

CHAPTER 34

Victorious Return to Political Roots

Addie and supporters celebrate her return

My Final Chapter

At the end of my term as county commissioner, I returned to my political roots and was again elected to the Mangonia Park Town Council.

After serving two years, I decided to seek re-election for another two years. Only this time, a newcomer, Kelisha Buchanan-Webb, became my opponent. She and I were eventually in a run-off. On March 11, 2010, Kelisha Webb was victorious with ninety votes to my eighty one.

After my defeat, my minister, Reverend Gerald D. Kisner telephoned me.

"Sister Greene," he said, "as a survivor, your health is very important to us. You should be enjoying your retirement, relaxing and finishing your book."

"Reverend Kisner," I said, "'thanks to you, that is exactly what I have done!"

About the Author

Brains. Beauty. Change Agent. Fighter. Politician. Educator. Activist. These are just a few words that describe the immensely, talented Addie Greene.

Addie L. Greene was born in Black Creek, Alabama. She received her B.S. Degree from Stillman College in Tuscaloosa, Alabama and her Master's Degree from Florida A & M University. She began her teaching career in the Glades at the following schools: Lake Shore Jr. Sr. High School, East Lake Jr. Sr. High School and Pahokee High School where students elected her Pahokee's first Black "Teacher of the Year."

After the Glades, she taught English at Boca Raton High School and John F. Kennedy Jr Sr. High School. In 1977, Addie left the public school system and became a Communications Instructor at Palm Beach Junior college, where she remained for twenty-seven (27) years.

In 1983, she began her political career in the Town of Mangonia Park as the first African American female Councilperson, where she later became the Vice Mayor and finally the Mayor. In 1992, Addie Greene was the first Black elected to the Florida House of Representatives from Palm Beach County. Addie L. Greene retired as the County Commissioner April 30, 2009.In 2011, she returned to politics to become elected again to the Mangonia Park Town Council. She finally retired in 2012.

Because of term limits, she left the Florida State Legislature in 2000 and was elected as a Palm Beach County Commissioner for District 7. She served nine (9) years and served as Chair for two years.

Her accolades are numerous. She ran out of wall space for the many impressive and well-deserved awards she has received over the years.

Addie L. Greene has truly come from the coal mines to the Boardroom.

QUESTIONS: FROM THE COAL MINES TO THE BOARD ROOM

1. Define government subsidies.
2. What is a shot-gun house?
3. How did coal miners use scrip or clacker?
4. When was scrip or clacker outlawed?
5. Why did Gov. George Wallace block entrance of Ms. Vivian Malone to the Univ. of Alabama?
6. Name some teachers who began their teaching careers in the Glades.
7. Name the first black Pahokee High School teacher of the year.
8. Who was Mrs. Stebbins Freddie Jefferson?
9. Name the first black female elected mayor of the Town of Mangonia Park?
10. Define redistricting.
11. What is Dr. Gerald C. Burke well-known for among PBC educators?
12. Define caucus.
13. How many persons make up the Florida House of Representatives?
14. How many persons make up the Florida Senate? Who is your Senator?
15. Who is your Congressperson?
16. Name the first African American Mayors of Belle Glade, South Bay, and Clewiston.
17. What position did Diane Walker hold before becoming a Pahokee Commissioner?
18. What was the Rosewood Massacre?
19. What is the name Alberta Birdie Burden known for?
20. Why did PBC state attorney Barry Krishner ask the State Legislature to pass a law to establish a law for a Victim Witness Protection Program?
21. Who is Maude Ford Lee?
22. Name the mayors of the following cities in 2000? Riviera Beach, Delray Beach, Lantana, Boynton Beach, Palm Beach, Lake Worth, Lake Park, Royal Palm Beach and Mangonia Park, Hypoluxo
23. Name the first African American minister elected mayor of the City of Riviera Beach.
24. Who founded the Palm Beach County Caucus of Black Elected officials?
25. Who were the two consultants to the Black Elected Officials?
26. What political position did Attorney Mack Bernard hold before he became District 7 County Commissioner?
27. What political position did Attorney Al Jacquet hold before he became a state Legislator?
28. What political position does Mr. Bobby Powell hold?
29. Name the accounting Firm that represented the Palm Beach County Caucus of Black Elected Officials.
30. Name the two African American School Board Members.
31. Name two African American West Palm Beach City Commissioners?
32. Name the African American Palm Beach County Port Commissioners.
33. What is Scripps Research Institute? Where is it located?
34. List the members of Commissioner Addie Greene's "Think Tank."
35. Why was Paragon Florida formed?
36. Who is Dr. Dennis Gallon?
37. Name the longest serving City commissioner in the history of the West Palm Beach.
38. Name the Haverhill council members.

See Answers on Back

ANSWERS: FROM THE COAL MINES TO THE BOARD ROOM

1. Anything that is paid for by the government.
2. a narrow rectangular residence with rooms one behind the other and doors at each end of the house.
3. Scrip or clacker was used to purchase goods at the company store.
4. In the 1950's
5. To prevent the integration of the University of Alabama
6. Addie L. Greene, Dr. Gerald Burke, Mrs. Freddie Jefferson
7. Addie Greene- Lincoln
8. Palm Beach Post columnist, retired teacher, communist activist.
9. Addie L. Greene
10. The process of by which congress and the state legislature draw district boundaries every ten years.
11. A legendary, well-known educator who assisted hundred of beginning educators.
12. A group of people with shared concerns within a political group or party
13. 120
14. 40
15. Congressman Alcee Hastings or Congresswoman Lois Frankel, etc
16. Mayor Steve Wilson
17. Secretary to Representative Addie L. Greene (The Pahokee Office).
18. In 1923, a white woman was beaten and residents of Sumner, Florida claimed her assailant was black, which caused race riots and the black town of Rosewood was burned down while the law enforcement looked the other way.
19. The Victim Witness Protection program
20. To protect victim and witnesses to a crime with tax payers funds
21. The first black elected to the Palm Beach County Commission
22. Riviera Beach - Mayor Michael Brown, Mangonia Park - Mayor William Albury, Delray Beach - Woodie Duffie, Royal Palm Beach - Mayor Fred Pinto, Lantana - David Stewart, Lake Park - Desca DuBois, Boynton - David Broening, Boynton Beach - Jose Rodriques, Palm Beach - Gail Coniglio, Lake Worth - Rene Varela, Hypoluxo - Kenneth Shultz
23. Mayor Thomas Masters
24. Addie L. Greene
25. Mrs. Mami Kisner and Mrs. Sandra Bridges
26. State Representative -District 84
27. Delray Beach Commissioner
28. State Senator
29. Zenora Ward, CPA
30. Dr. Debra Robinson and Marcia Andrews
31. West Palm Beach Commissioners Corey Neering and Keith James
32. Port Commissioners Dr. Jean Enright and Attorney Wayne Richards
33. A medical facility that focuses on research and education in the biomedical sciences. It is located in Jupiter, Florida
34. Clarence Anthony, Mami Kisner, Roy Mouton (Deceased), Paul Nunnally, William Albury and Dr. Debra Robinson
35. To provide comprehensive loan programs, training and management and technical assistance to minority businesses in Palm Beach County
36. Former and first black president of Palm Beach State College
37. Former Commissioner Isaac Robinson
38. Haverhill Mayor Jay Foy, Vice Mayor Lawrence Gordon, Council members Remar Harvin, Daniel H. Sohn, and Mark C. Uptegraph

www.ingramcontent.com/pod-product-compliance
Lightning Source LLC
Chambersburg PA
CBHW042128160426
43198CB00021B/2939